BASICS OF PREPRESS: A COMPREHENSIVE GUIDE

Edition 1
Published on 2024

SHERIFF BLATHUR
Printing & Packaging Expert

Basics of Prepress
A Comprehensive Guide
Sheriff Blathur

Published by White Falcon Publishing
Chandigarh, India

ISBN - 979-8-89222-407-9

PREFACE

"BASICS OF PREPRESS: A COMPREHENSIVE GUIDE" serves as an essential reference for students in printing and graphic design, as well as for beginners entering the graphic design field. This guide provides a detailed overview of the entire prepress process, making it an invaluable resource for anyone looking to understand the intricacies involved in preparing digital files for printing.

The book covers various stages of the prepress workflow, from initial design concepts to the final steps before printing. It includes topics such as:

- **Design Fundamentals**: Understanding the principles of design, including layout, typography, and color theory.
- **Software Proficiency**: Guidance on using industry-standard software tools like Adobe InDesign, Illustrator, and Photoshop.
- **File Preparation**: Instructions on how to properly prepare digital files, ensuring they meet the technical specifications required for high-quality printing.
- **Proofing and Adjustments**: Techniques for proofing and making necessary adjustments to ensure accuracy and consistency in the final print.
- **Color Management**: An in-depth look at color theory, color spaces, and color correction to achieve the desired outcome in printed materials.
- **Printing Techniques**: An overview of different printing methods, such as offset, digital, and screen printing, and how to prepare files for each.
- **Prepress Technology**: Introduction to the technology and equipment used in the prepress stage, including scanners, RIPs (Raster Image Processors), and platemaking.

By following the guidance provided in this book, readers will gain a comprehensive understanding of the prepress process. This knowledge will equip them with the skills needed to become efficient and effective prepress executives or managers. The book emphasizes practical, real-world applications and includes tips for troubleshooting common issues, ensuring that readers can confidently handle the entire prepress process with a small amount of industrial exposure.

Whether you are a student aspiring to enter the printing and graphic design industry or a beginner seeking to enhance your prepress skills, "BASICS OF PREPRESS: A COMPREHENSIVE GUIDE" is the ultimate resource for mastering the prepress workflow and excelling in your career.

ABOUT THE AUTHOR:

This book has been written by Muhammed Sheriff known as Sheriff Blathur from Kerala State of India. With over 11 years of experience in the printing and packaging industry, he is a Prepress In Charge at Balmer Lawrie UAE LLC, a leading company in the field of industrial packaging and printing. He has very good exposure to Flexo, Offset, Gravure, and Digital Printing Technologies.

He has a strong background in color management, having worked with Fogra and G7 standards and tools, as well as the PepsiCo Graphics Quality Program by Xrite. He has also managed and supervised teams of designers and prepress operators, and supported and facilitated the press and postpress operations.

He completed a B.Tech in Printing Technology from Calicut University Institute of Engineering and Technology and obtained a certification in Packaging Science from the Indian Institute of Packaging as a 'Certified Packaging Engineer'.

TABLE OF CONTENTS:

Chapter 12: Future Trends in Prepress

Glossary

Appendices

1. INTRODUCTION TO PREPRESS

1.1 Understanding Prepress

Definition and Scope Prepress encompasses all the steps and processes that occur after a design is created but before it is printed. This phase is critical in ensuring that the final printed product meets the desired quality and specifications.

Historical Context Prepress has evolved significantly over the years. Traditionally, it involved manual processes like typesetting and plate making. With the advent of digital technologies, the prepress phase now includes advanced software and automated systems that streamline and enhance the workflow.

Key Components of Prepress

- **File Preparation**: Ensuring the digital files are print-ready.
- **Proofing**: Creating proofs to check for errors.
- **Color Management**: Adjusting and managing colors to match the final output.
- **Imposition**: Arranging pages for efficient printing.
- **Preflighting**: Checking files for potential print issues.
- **Trapping**: Adjusting overlapping colors to prevent gaps.
- **RIP**: Converting files into a format that the printer can use.

1.2 The Importance of Prepress in the Printing Industry

Quality Assurance The prepress process is crucial for maintaining high print quality. By meticulously checking and preparing files, prepress ensures that the final output is free from errors and meets the design specifications.

Cost Efficiency Identifying and correcting issues during the prepress stage prevents costly mistakes during the printing phase. This reduces waste and saves time and resources.

Consistency and Reliability Prepress ensures consistency across different print runs, which is vital for brand integrity. Accurate color management and proofing help maintain the same appearance across multiple prints.

Client Satisfaction A thorough prepress process results in a high-quality final product, which leads to greater client satisfaction. Meeting and exceeding client expectations is essential for building and maintaining strong business relationships.

1.3 Overview of the Prepress Workflow

Step-by-Step Breakdown

1. **File Preparation**
   - Convert files to the correct format (e.g., PDF).
   - Check resolution, color modes, and file dimensions.
   - Ensure all fonts and images are embedded.
2. **Preflighting**
   - Use software to scan files for common issues (e.g., low resolution, missing fonts).
   - Generate a preflight report highlighting any problems.
3. **Proofing**
   - Create digital proofs for initial review.
   - Produce hard copy proofs if needed for color accuracy.
   - Review proofs with the client and make necessary adjustments.
4. **Color Management**
   - Apply appropriate color profiles.

- o Calibrate monitors and printers to ensure color consistency.
  - o Adjust colors to match the intended output.
5. **Imposition**
  - o Arrange pages on the printer's sheet to maximize efficiency.
  - o Consider the binding and cutting process to ensure proper order.
6. **Trapping**
  - o Adjust overlapping colors to account for misregistration.
  - o Use software tools to automate trapping where possible.
7. **RIP (Raster Image Processor)**
  - o Convert vector graphics and text into a raster image.
  - o Prepare the final file for the printing press.
8. **Final Output**
  - o Perform a final check of the prepared files.
  - o Communicate with the printer to confirm specifications.
  - o Send files to the printer for production.

Tools and Software Prepress involves a variety of specialized software tools, including:

- Adobe Creative Suite (Illustrator, InDesign, Photoshop)
- Preflight software (e.g., Enfocus PitStop)
- Proofing tools (e.g., GMG ColorProof)
- Imposition software (e.g., Kodak Preps)
- RIP software (e.g., EFI Fiery)

Roles and Responsibilities The prepress process often involves collaboration between different professionals, such as:

- Graphic Designers: Create and finalize the design files.

- Prepress Technicians: Prepare and check files for print readiness.
- Proofreaders: Review content for errors.
- Color Specialists: Manage color consistency and accuracy.
- Print Operators: Execute the final printing process.

By understanding and mastering the prepress process, professionals in the printing industry can ensure high-quality, cost-effective, and consistent print products that meet client expectations.

2. FILE PREPARATION

2.1 Designing for Print vs. Digital

Understanding the Differences Designing for print and designing for digital platforms require different considerations due to the distinct nature of each medium.

Print Design

- **Resolution**: Requires higher resolution (300 dpi or more) to ensure clarity and detail in the printed material.
- **Color Mode**: Uses CMYK (Cyan, Magenta, Yellow, Black) for color reproduction.
- **Physical Dimensions**: Must account for the physical size of the printed piece and incorporate bleed and trim areas.
- **File Formats**: Common formats include PDF, TIFF, and EPS.
- **Typography**: Must ensure that fonts are embedded or outlined to prevent missing font issues.

Digital Design

- **Resolution**: Typically lower resolution (72 dpi) is sufficient for screens.
- **Color Mode**: Uses RGB (Red, Green, Blue) for screen display.
- **Scalability**: Needs to be responsive and scalable to different screen sizes.
- **File Formats**: Common formats include JPEG, PNG, GIF, and SVG.
- **Interactivity**: May include interactive elements like hyperlinks, animations, and video.

Key Considerations for Print Design

- **Print Readiness**: Ensuring the design is suitable for print, with correct dimensions and bleed.
- **Font Management**: Embedding or converting fonts to outlines to avoid issues.
- **Image Quality**: Using high-resolution images to maintain print quality.
- **Proofing**: Reviewing digital and hard copy proofs to catch errors.

2.2 Resolution and Image Quality

Understanding Resolution

- **DPI vs. PPI**: Dots per inch (DPI) is used for print, while pixels per inch (PPI) is used for digital images.
- **High Resolution**: Essential for print to ensure clarity and sharpness (300 dpi is standard for most print jobs).

Image Quality

- **Vector vs. Raster**: Vector graphics are scalable without loss of quality, while raster images can become pixelated when scaled.
- **Image Compression**: Avoid excessive compression to prevent quality loss. Use lossless formats like TIFF for print.

Best Practices

- **Scanning Images**: Scan at a high resolution (300 dpi or higher) for print.
- **Editing**: Perform image editing in high resolution to maintain quality.

- **Resampling**: Avoid upscaling images; if necessary, use software with advanced resampling algorithms.

2.3 Color Modes: RGB vs. CMYK

Color Theory

- **RGB Color Model**: Used for digital displays. Colors are created by combining red, green, and blue light (Picture 1).
- **CMYK Color Model**: Used for print. Colors are created by combining cyan, magenta, yellow, and black ink (Picture 1).

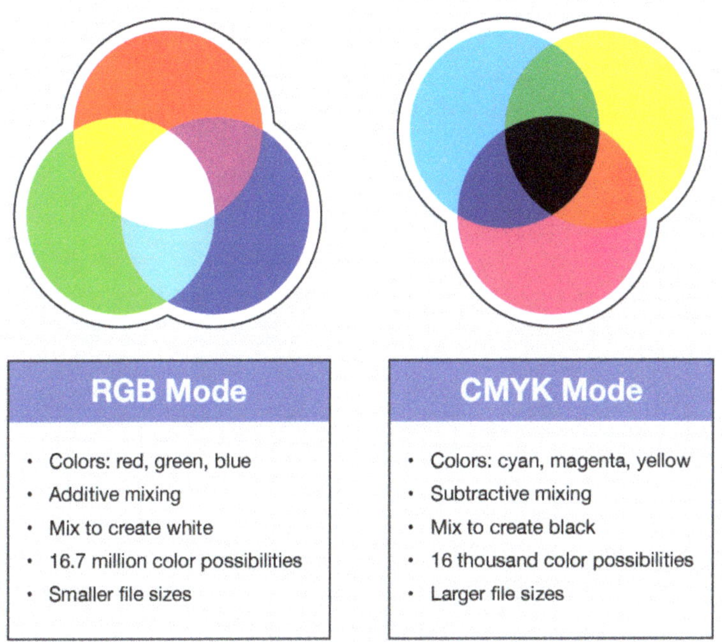

Picture 1: RGB and CMYK Color Spaces

Conversion and Consistency

Designing in RGB: Many design tools default to RGB. Conversion to CMYK is necessary for print, but this can cause color shifts.

- **Soft Proofing**: Use soft proofing tools to simulate how RGB colors will look when converted to CMYK.
- **Color Profiles**: Apply appropriate ICC profiles to ensure accurate color reproduction during the conversion process.

Profiles used for creating files are crucial. In Europe, the Middle East, and North Africa, the common CMYK profiles for sheet-fed offset printing are Coated Fogra 39 or Fogra 51. In the US, brand owners and the sheet-fed offset printers typically use Gracol 2007 or Gracol 2013 profiles. It's essential to embed the profile into the file to ensure that viewers or editors adhere to the same profile in subsequent processes.

Common Pitfalls

- **Color Shifts**: Be aware that vibrant RGB colors may not have a direct CMYK equivalent, leading to duller prints. Therefore, it is always advised to work in CMYK mode
- **Gamut Issues**: RGB has a wider color gamut than CMYK, meaning some colors can't be reproduced in print. Because of that, some colors have been printed as spot colors or Pantone Colors to get the exact reproduction. Also, the six color printing or seven color printing (also called OGV Printing or extended Gamut Printing) is used to enhance the gamut to get the exact color reproduction. Here Orange, Green and Violet inks have been used along with CMYK. (Picture 2)
- **Substrate Variation**: Same color combination will be reproduced into different shades when we are using different types of substrates. Physical, chemical and optical properties will affect the printability of the substrate. Standard substrate can be used for getting color consistency. Custom profiles can

be made and applied for customized or non-standard substrates.

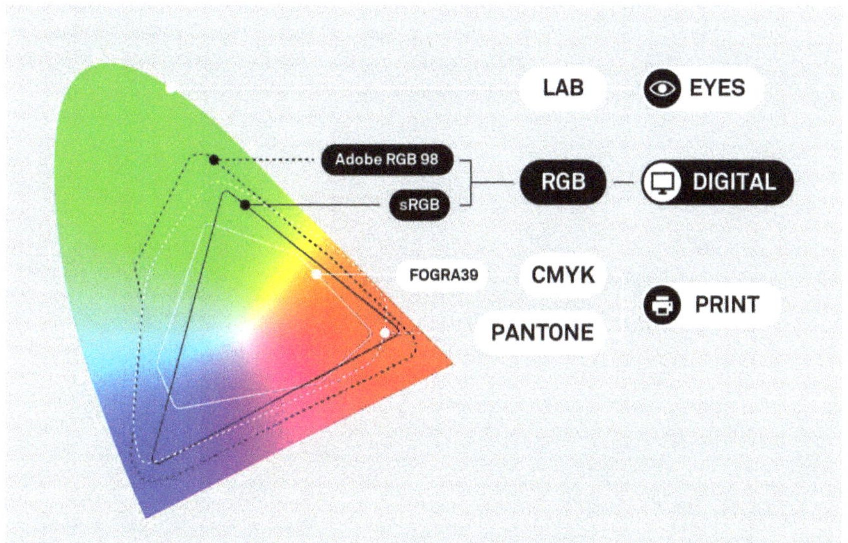

Picture 2. Pictorial Representation of Different Color Gamuts

2.4 Bleed, Trim, and Safe Areas

Bleed

- **Definition**: The area beyond the trim edge where the design extends to prevent white borders after trimming.
- **Standard Bleed Size**: Typically 1/8 inch (3mm) on all sides, but can vary based on the printer's requirements.

Trim

- **Definition**: The final size of the printed piece after excess edges are cut off.

- **Trim Marks**: Indicate where the paper should be cut.

Safe Areas

- **Definition**: The area inside the trim where important content should be placed to avoid being cut off.
- **Margin Recommendations**: Keep crucial elements like text and logos at least 1/8 inch (3mm) away from the trim line.

Practical Tips

- **Design with Bleed**: Always include bleed in your design files to avoid unexpected white edges.
- **Use Guides**: Set up guides for bleed, trim, and safe areas in your design software to ensure accuracy.

2.5 File Formats and Compatibility

Common File Formats

- **PDF**: Preferred format for print due to its ability to embed fonts, images, and maintain layout integrity.
- **TIFF**: High-quality raster format, suitable for images and graphics.
- **EPS**: Vector format often used for logos and illustrations.
- **JPEG**: Compressed format, not ideal for print due to potential quality loss, but sometimes used for photos.
- **AI and PSD**: Native formats for Adobe Illustrator and Photoshop, often used during the design phase.

File Compatibility

- **Embedded Elements**: Ensure all fonts and images are embedded or outlined.
- **Preflighting**: Use preflight tools to check for compatibility issues before sending files to the printer.

- **Export Settings**: Use appropriate settings for exporting files to ensure they meet the printer's specifications.

Best Practices

- **Consistent Naming Conventions**: Use clear and consistent file naming to avoid confusion.
- **Version Control**: Keep track of different file versions to avoid using outdated files.
- **Backup Files**: Regularly back up your files to prevent data loss.

By adhering to these principles and best practices, designers can ensure their files are print-ready, minimizing errors and ensuring a smooth transition from digital design to physical print.

3. TYPOGRAPHY AND FONTS

Typography plays a crucial role in design, whether for print or digital media. Proper font selection, management, and typesetting are essential to ensure that your design communicates effectively and looks professional.

3.1 Choosing the Right Fonts

Understanding Font Types

- **Serif Fonts**: These fonts have small lines or strokes regularly attached to the end of a larger stroke in a letter or symbol. They are often used in print for body text due to their readability and traditional appearance (e.g., Times New Roman, Garamond). (Picture 3)

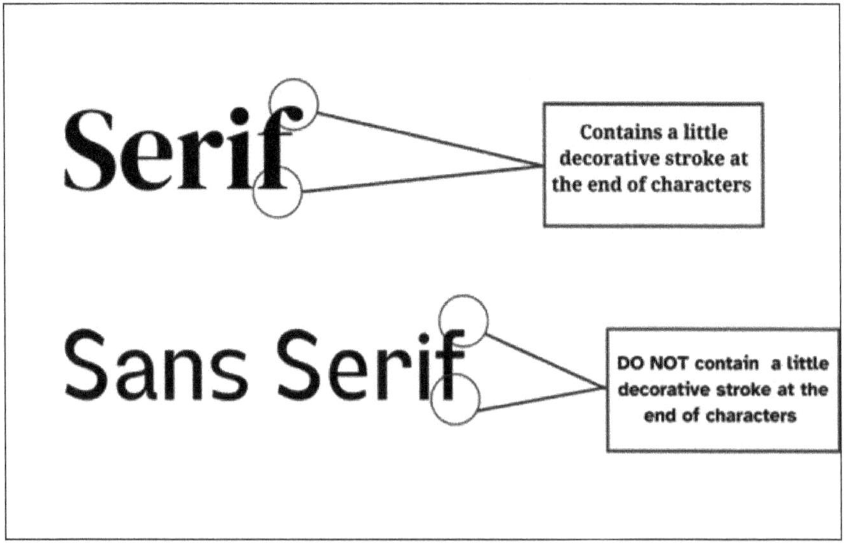

Picture 3. Serif and Sans Serif Fonts

- **Sans-Serif Fonts**: These fonts lack the small lines at the end of strokes. They are considered modern and clean, making them popular for both print headlines and digital use (e.g., Arial, Helvetica). (Picture 3)
- **Script Fonts**: Designed to resemble handwritten text, script fonts can add a personal or elegant touch to a design. They should be used sparingly and are best for decorative elements rather than body text (e.g., Brush Script, Pacifico). (Picture 4)

Picture 4. Script font sample

- **Display Fonts**: These are intended for large headings and should capture attention. They are often stylized and not suitable for body text due to their readability at smaller sizes (e.g., Impact, Lobster).

Key Considerations for Font Selection

- **Readability**: Choose fonts that are easy to read, especially for body text. Consider the size, weight, and spacing of the font.
- **Brand Consistency**: Fonts should align with the brand's identity. Consistent use of fonts across all materials helps reinforce the brand.
- **Purpose and Tone**: Select fonts that match the purpose and tone of your project. A formal document might require a serif font, while a modern website might use a sans-serif font.

- **Pairing Fonts**: When using multiple fonts, ensure they complement each other. A common approach is to pair a serif font with a sans-serif font to create contrast and visual interest.

3.2 Font Management and Embedding

Managing Fonts

- **Font Libraries**: Organize your fonts using font management software like Adobe Fonts, Google Fonts, or FontBase. These tools help you preview, categorize, and activate/deactivate fonts as needed.
- **Licensing**: Ensure you have the proper licenses for all fonts used in your projects. Many fonts require a license for commercial use.

Embedding Fonts

- **Print Design**: Embedding fonts in your design files (such as PDFs) ensures that they will appear correctly when printed. This prevents font substitution, which can alter the appearance of your text.
- **Digital Design**: For web use, include web-safe fonts or use web font services like Google Fonts to ensure consistency across different devices and browsers.

Best Practices

- **Convert to Outlines**: In vector-based design software (like Adobe Illustrator), converting text to outlines can prevent font issues. This process turns text into vector shapes, ensuring it looks exactly as intended. (Picture 5)
- **Include Font Files**: When sending design files to a printer or collaborator, include the font files or specify where the fonts can be downloaded.

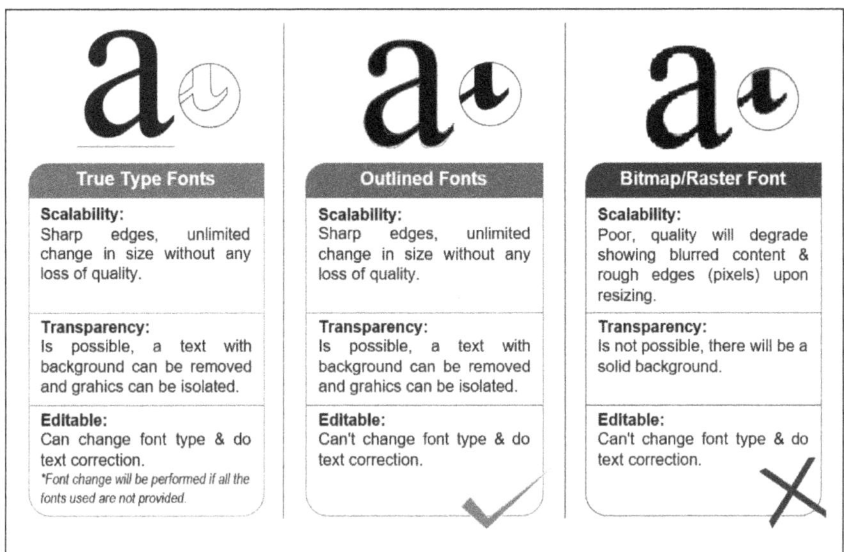

Picture 5. Different mode of fonts in files

3.3 Dealing with Missing Fonts

Identifying Missing Fonts

- **Preflighting**: Use preflight tools in design software to check for missing fonts before exporting or printing your files. This process identifies any font issues and allows you to correct them before finalizing the design.
- **Alerts**: Design software typically alerts you if fonts used in the document are not installed on your system. Take these alerts seriously and address them immediately.

Solutions for Missing Fonts

- **Replace Fonts**: If a font is missing and cannot be obtained, replace it with a similar font. Ensure the new font maintains the design's aesthetic and readability.

- **Embed Fonts**: Ensure that fonts are embedded in the file to avoid missing font issues when the file is opened on another computer.
- **Font Substitution**: Some software offers font substitution, which replaces the missing font with a similar one from the system. This is a last resort, as it can alter the design's appearance.

Preventive Measures

- **Font Documentation**: Keep a record of all fonts used in a project, including their sources and licenses. This makes it easier to address missing fonts if they occur.
- **Package Files**: When sharing files, use the packaging feature in design software to include all fonts, images, and other necessary files. This ensures everything needed to open and edit the file is included.

3.4 Kerning, Leading, and Tracking

Kerning

- **Definition**: Kerning refers to the adjustment of space between individual characters in a word. Proper kerning ensures that letters are spaced evenly and improves the overall appearance and readability of text. (Picture 6)
- **Manual vs. Automatic Kerning**: Some fonts include built-in kerning pairs that adjust automatically. However, manual adjustments may be necessary for headlines or decorative text.

Leading

- **Definition**: Leading (pronounced "ledding") is the vertical space between lines of text. Proper leading ensures that text is readable and aesthetically pleasing. (Picture 6)

- **Adjusting Leading**: Increase leading for better readability, especially in body text. Tight leading may be used for headlines to create a compact and bold look.

Tracking

- **Definition**: Tracking refers to the uniform adjustment of spacing between all characters in a block of text. It differs from kerning, which adjusts space between individual characters. (Picture 6)

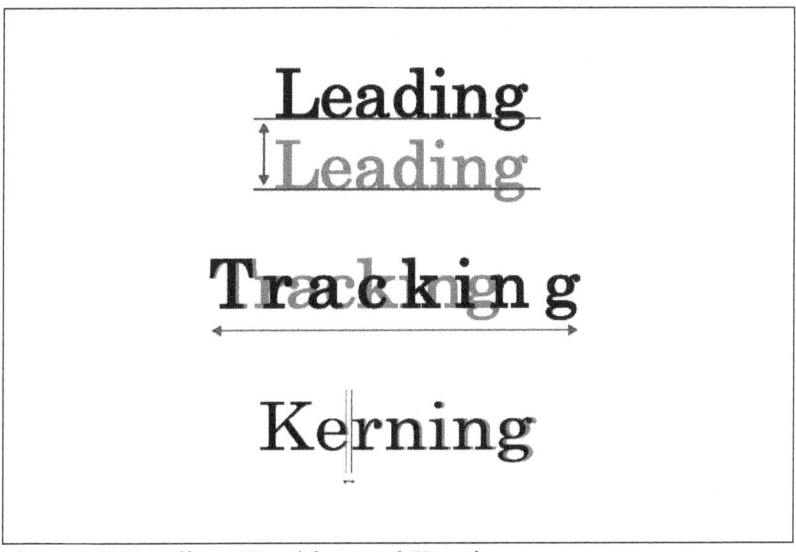

Picture 6. Leading, Tracking and Kerning

- **Applications**: Adjust tracking to improve readability or achieve a specific visual effect. Tight tracking can create a dense, bold appearance, while loose tracking can create an airy, open feel.

Best Practices

- **Consistency**: Maintain consistent kerning, leading, and tracking throughout your design to ensure a cohesive and professional look.

- **Readability**: Prioritize readability, especially for body text. Adjust spacing to ensure that text is easy to read at the intended size.
- **Visual Balance**: Use kerning, leading, and tracking to achieve visual balance in your design. Proper spacing can enhance the overall aesthetic and make the text more engaging.

By understanding and applying these principles of typography, designers can create visually appealing and readable designs that effectively communicate their intended message. Proper font selection, management, and typesetting are essential skills for any designer working in print or digital media.

4. PROOFING

Proofing is a critical step in the prepress process that ensures your design will look as intended when printed. It involves reviewing and making necessary adjustments to your files before they go to the printer, thus minimizing errors and avoiding costly reprints.

4.1 The Proofing Process

What is Proofing? Proofing is the process of creating a prototype or sample of the final printed piece to review for errors and make necessary adjustments. It serves as the last line of defense before a project goes to print, ensuring that the design meets quality standards and is free of errors.

Steps in the Proofing Process

1. **Initial Review**: After completing the design, review the file for any obvious errors in layout, typography, images, and colors.
2. **Create a Proof**: Generate a proof using proofing software or hardware. This can be a digital proof (soft proof) or a physical proof (hard proof).
3. **Detailed Inspection**: Carefully inspect the proof for issues such as color accuracy, image resolution, font consistency, alignment, and any potential printing problems.
4. **Make Adjustments**: Correct any identified issues in the original design file. Repeat the proofing process as needed until the proof is error-free.
5. **Final Approval**: Once the proof meets all standards and requirements, approve the proof for printing.

Proofing Checklist

- **Spelling and Grammar**: Check for typos and grammatical errors.
- **Images and Graphics**: Ensure all images are high resolution and correctly placed.
- **Colors**: Verify that colors are accurate and consistent with brand guidelines.
- **Layout and Alignment**: Check that all elements are properly aligned and spaced.
- **Bleed and Trim**: Ensure bleed and trim areas are correctly set up to prevent white edges or cut-off elements.

4.2 Types of Proofs: Soft Proofs vs. Hard Proofs

Soft Proofs

- **Definition**: A soft proof is a digital version of the final product viewed on a screen. It allows for a quick and cost-effective way to review the design.
- **Advantages**:
  - Instantaneous review and feedback.
  - Lower cost since no physical materials are needed.
  - Easy to share with remote clients and team members.
- **Disadvantages**:
  - Color accuracy may vary depending on the monitor's calibration.
  - Screen resolution can differ from print resolution, affecting detail perception.
  - Not suitable for final approval of color-critical projects.

Hard Proofs

- **Definition**: A hard proof is a physical print of the final design. It is created using the same or similar process as the final print run.
- **Advantages**:
  - Accurate representation of colors, textures, and finishes.
  - Helps identify issues with paper choice and print quality.
  - Provides a tangible sample for client approval.
- **Disadvantages**:
  - Higher cost due to printing and materials.
  - Longer turnaround time compared to digital proofs.
  - Less convenient for remote approval.

When to Use Each Type

- **Soft Proofs**: Ideal for initial reviews, digital projects, and when budget or time constraints are a concern.
- **Hard Proofs**: Essential for final approval, color-critical projects, and when the physical appearance of the print matters.

4.3 Reviewing and Approving Proofs

Review Process

- **Initial Check**: Conduct an initial review to identify any glaring issues. This can be done individually or in a team setting.
- **Detailed Review**: Perform a meticulous review of the proof, checking all elements against the original design specifications and brand guidelines.

- **Client Feedback**: If applicable, share the proof with clients for their review and feedback. Ensure they understand the proofing process and what to look for.
- **Iterative Proofing**: Make necessary corrections based on feedback and create new proofs as needed until all parties are satisfied.

Approval Process

- **Internal Approval**: Obtain approval from all internal stakeholders, such as designers, project managers, and brand managers.
- **Client Approval**: Secure final approval from the client. Ensure they have reviewed and signed off on all aspects of the proof, including color, layout, and text.
- **Documentation**: Keep detailed records of all feedback, changes made, and approvals received. This documentation can be crucial in case of disputes or issues later on.

Best Practices

- **Clear Communication**: Maintain clear and open communication with all parties involved in the proofing process. Ensure everyone understands their role and responsibilities.
- **Standardized Procedures**: Establish and follow standardized proofing procedures to ensure consistency and accuracy.
- **Training**: Train team members on how to properly review and approve proofs to minimize errors.

4.4 Common Proofing Errors and How to Avoid Them

Common Errors

- **Color Inconsistencies**: Colors in the final print may differ from the design due to incorrect color profiles or monitor calibration.
- **Low-Resolution Images**: Using images that are not high enough resolution can result in pixelation and poor print quality. The preflighting software can detect this problem but it cannot fix this issue.
- **Typography Issues**: Missing fonts, incorrect font usage, or typographical errors can affect the final print.
- **Layout Shifts**: Elements may shift during the proofing process, resulting in misaligned or improperly spaced designs.
- **Incorrect Bleed and Trim**: Failing to include proper bleed and trim areas can result in unwanted white edges or cut-off elements.

How to Avoid Them

- **Color Management**: It is very important to use an appropriate and constant profile across the workflow according to the final output. Then only we will get a consistent output from the production run. A standard CMYK frofile should be used for print jobs and a standard RGB profile should be used for web / visual media. Use calibrated monitors to get a consistent and proper reproduction of the color. Soft proof using software that can simulate the print output.
- **High-Resolution Images**: Ensure all images are at least 300 dpi for print. Check image resolution during the initial design phase and before proofing.
- **Font Management**: Embed fonts in design files and convert text to outlines if necessary. Double-check for missing fonts

during the preflight process. Free fonts can be downloaded and install to solve this issue. Fonts can be identified by using online font finder platforms such as "What the font is", "Find My Fonts", etc.

- **Consistent Layouts**: Lock elements in place in design software and double-check alignment and spacing before creating a proof.
- **Proper Bleed and Trim**: Set up bleed and trim areas according to printer specifications. Use design software guides to ensure all elements are within safe areas. (Picture 7)

By following these guidelines and best practices, designers can minimize errors and ensure their projects are print-ready, ultimately leading to a smoother printing process and a high-quality final product.

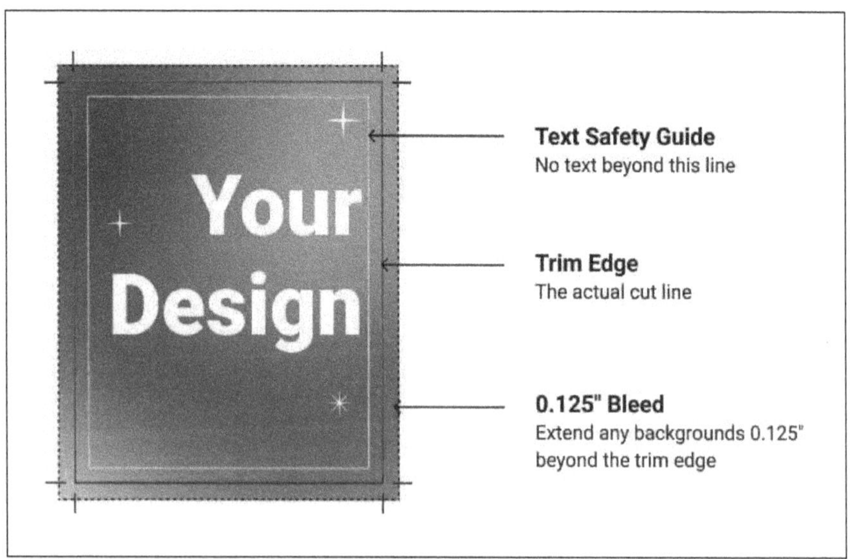

Picture 7. Bleed, Trim & Safety Boxes

5. COLOR MANAGEMENT

5.1 Understanding Color Theory

Color theory is the foundation of color management. It encompasses the principles and guidelines regarding how colors interact, how they are perceived by the human eye, and how they can be combined to create visually appealing compositions.

- **Primary Colors**: The basic colors that cannot be created by mixing other colors. In the RGB color model (used in digital displays), these are Red, Green, and Blue. In the CMYK color model (used in printing), they are Cyan, Magenta, Yellow, and Black.
- **Secondary Colors**: Created by mixing two primary colors. For RGB, these are Cyan, Magenta, and Yellow. For CMYK, secondary colors can include Orange, Green, and Purple.
- **Tertiary Colors**: Created by mixing a primary and a secondary color.
- **Color Wheel**: A circular diagram representing the relationships between colors. It is used to identify harmonious color combinations (analogous, complementary, triadic).
- **Color Harmony**: Techniques for creating aesthetically pleasing color combinations. These include complementary (opposite colors on the color wheel), analogous (colors next to each other), and triadic (three colors evenly spaced).
- **Color Temperature**: Describes the warmth or coolness of a color. Warm colors (reds, oranges) are associated with sunlight, while cool colors (blues, greens) are associated with shade.

5.2 Color Profiles and ICC Profiles

In the world of graphic reproduction, color is paramount. It can convey emotion, create visual interest, and define a brand's identity.

However, achieving the exact color you envision isn't as straightforward as choosing from a palette. Color profiles, often overlooked by many designers, play a critical role in ensuring the colors you see on your screen match what appears in print. Simply put, a color profile is the language of color. Without understanding this language, translating colors accurately across different devices and media can be challenging.

- **Color Profiles**: Data sets that describe the color attributes of a particular device or viewing condition. They ensure that the colors are represented accurately.
- **ICC Profiles**: A standard set by the International Color Consortium (ICC) to create device-independent color profiles. ICC profiles help in the accurate translation of colors from one device to another.
- **Device-Specific Profiles**: Profiles tailored to specific devices like monitors, printers, and scanners. These profiles ensure that the colors displayed or printed match the intended design.
- **Embedding Profiles**: The process of including a color profile within a digital file (e.g., an image or PDF) to maintain color accuracy across different devices and software.

The Importance of Color Profiles

Color profiles are standardized sets of data that dictate how colors should appear on various devices, such as monitors, printers, and cameras. When you don't know the specific color profile in which a file is created, significant color variations can occur during the transition from digital design to printed material. This can lead to disappointing results, where the printed colors differ greatly from the designer's intent.

Common Color Profiles in Use

Despite their importance, about 95% of graphic designers are unaware of which color settings they use in Adobe Illustrator. This lack of awareness can lead to inconsistencies, especially when working with different printing methods or geographical regions. For instance, many designers default to the "U.S. Web Coated (SWOP)" profile, which is intended for web offset printing in the United States. However, this profile isn't always suitable for other printing processes, such as sheet-fed offset printing.

Regional Preferences and Standards

Different regions around the world follow different color profile standards based on their printing practices and industry standards:

- **Middle East, Europe, and North Africa**: These regions predominantly use Fogra color settings. Introduced in 2007, the Coated Fogra 39 profile is widely used for general printing needs. For premium coated substrates, designers and printers often opt for the Fogra 51 profile, which offers more accurate color reproduction for high-end printing materials.
- **United States**: In the U.S., Gracol settings are the standard for sheet-fed offset jobs. The Gracol 2006 profile was commonly used until the introduction of the Gracol 2013 profile, which has since become the preferred choice for many brand owners and printers. These profiles ensure consistency and reliability in color reproduction, which is crucial for maintaining brand integrity.

Why Knowing Your Color Profile Matters

Understanding and selecting the correct color profile is essential for several reasons:

1. **Color Accuracy**: Ensuring that the colors you see on your screen match what appears in print.
2. **Consistency**: Maintaining uniformity across different print jobs and media, which is vital for brand recognition.
3. **Efficiency**: Reducing the need for multiple test prints and adjustments, saving time and resources.

Best Practices for Designers

To avoid color discrepancies and ensure the best possible results, designers should:

1. **Identify the Correct Profile**: Determine the appropriate color profile based on the printing process and geographic location.
2. **Calibrate Devices**: Regularly calibrate monitors and printers to ensure they are accurately displaying colors.
3. **Communicate with Printers**: Work closely with printers to understand their requirements and adjust settings accordingly.
4. **Stay Updated**: Keep abreast of industry standards and updates to color profiles, as these can change over time.

Color profiles are indeed the language of color in graphic design. Without a firm grasp of this language, translating colors accurately from digital design to printed material can be fraught with challenges. By understanding and correctly applying color profiles, designers can ensure their work looks as intended, regardless of the medium or region in which it is produced. As the saying goes, "If you don't know the language, the translation will be difficult." The same holds true for color profiles in graphic design.

5.3 Adobe Photoshop & Illustrator Color Settings

Open Color Settings:

- **Adobe Illustrator**: Go to `Edit > Color Settings`.
- **Adobe Photoshop**: Go to `Edit > Color Settings`.

Setting Up Color Profiles:

1. **Working Spaces**:
   - **RGB**:
     - Set to `Adobe RGB (1998)`. This profile offers a broader color gamut, ideal for images intended for print.
   - **CMYK**:
     - Select the appropriate profile based on your requirement:
     - **Fogra 39**: Set to `Coated Fogra 39`, a standard for offset printing. (Picture 8)
     - **Fogra 51**: Set to `PSO Coated v3`, used for improved print quality on modern substrates.
     - **GRACoL 2013**: Set to `GRACoL2013_CRPC6`, tailored for North American printing standards.
2. **Color Management Policies**:
   - **RGB**: Select `Preserve Embedded Profiles`. This ensures that the document retains its original color profile.
   - **CMYK**: Select `Preserve Embedded Profiles`. This maintains the integrity of the color data from the source.
   - **Gray**: Select `Preserve Embedded Profiles`. This is crucial for grayscale images to retain their intended look.

3. **Conversion Options**:
   - **Engine**: Set to `Adobe  (ACE)`. The Adobe Color Engine (ACE) ensures consistent color conversion across Adobe applications.
   -
   - **Intent**: Set to `Relative Colorimetric` and check the box for `Black Point Compensation`. This setting preserves the relative visual differences between colors and compensates for different black levels in source and destination profiles.

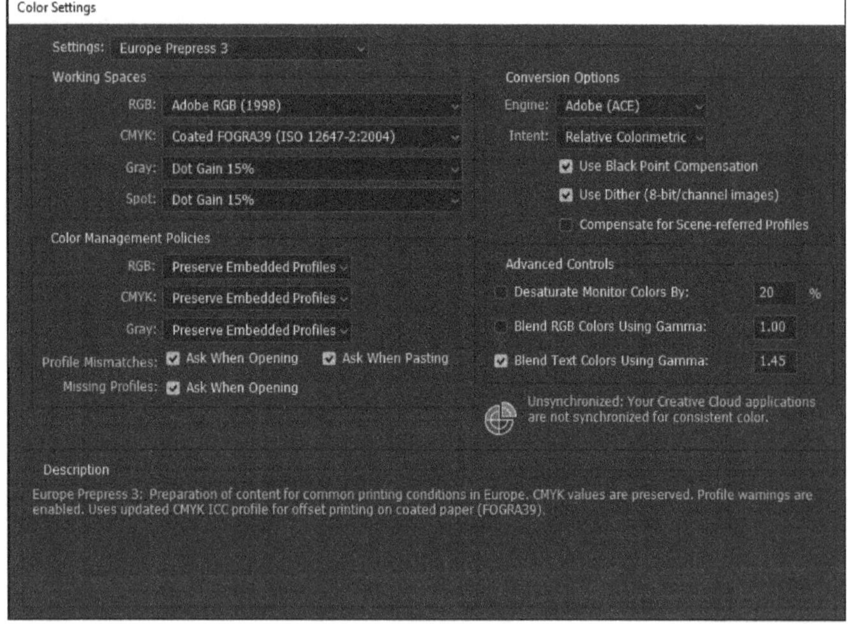

Picture 8. Adobe Photoshop Color Settings

4. **Advanced Controls**:
   - Leave these settings as default unless you have specific needs. These controls offer fine-tuning for color handling but are typically best left unchanged for general use.

5. **Save Color Settings**:
   - o Save these settings for future use by clicking `Save...`, then name the settings file. This allows you to load the same settings easily later. Synchronize these settings from Adobe Bridge so that all Adobe software will have the same color settings.

5.4 File Saving Options with PDF/X

It is crucial to save the file in a format that suits the final output of the job. Otherwise, there may be miscommunication and misunderstandings, leading to inconsistencies in the files.

Save As PDF:

- In Illustrator or Photoshop, go to `File` > `Save As` and choose `Adobe PDF (pdf)` as the file type.

PDF Preset:

- Select a PDF/X preset that matches your needs:
  - o **PDF/X-1a:2001**
  - o **PDF/X-3:2002**
  - o **PDF/X-4:2010** (Preferred for modern workflows)

PDF Options:

In the `Save Adobe PDF` dialog, configure the following settings:

1. **General**:
   - o Ensure `Preserve Illustrator Editing Capabilities` is unchecked (for smaller file size).
   - o Optionally, check `Optimize for Fast Web View`.
2. **Compression**:

o Set image quality according to the requirements (usually high or maximum). For offset jobs, there is no benefit in saving images with a resolution higher than 300ppi, as it is the maximum printing capacity. Similarly, for large format printing, a resolution of up to 75ppi is often sufficient. Saving files with higher resolutions than recommended can waste memory space and complicate file handling.

3. **Marks and Bleeds**:
   o Include necessary marks (crop marks, registration marks, etc.) and set the bleed values if required by your print specifications.

4. **Output**:
   o **Color Conversion**: Select `Convert to Destination`.
   o **Destination**: Select the appropriate profile (e.g., Fogra 39, Fogra 51, GRACoL 2013).
   o **Profile Inclusion Policy**: Set to `Include All Profiles`. This ensures the color profile is embedded in the PDF.

5. **Advanced**:
   o **Subset fonts when the percentage of characters used is less than**: Set to `100%`. This embeds only the characters used in the document, reducing file size.

6. **Security**:
   o Set password protection if needed (optional). This can prevent unauthorized editing or viewing of the document.

Embedding Profiles:

- Ensure that the `Output Intent Profile Name` matches the profile used (Fogra 39, Fogra 51, or GRACoL 2013). This ensures the profile is embedded in the PDF, guaranteeing accurate color reproduction.

5.5 Viewing Conditions in Adobe Acrobat Professional

When the file is opened in Adobe Acrobat Professional, it should automatically recognize the embedded profile and display colors correctly. However, it is also essential to ensure that you are viewing the file using the correct profile in the output preview of Adobe Acrobat Professional.

Here's how you can do that:

1. **Open the PDF**:
   o Open your PDF file in Adobe Acrobat Professional.
2. **Access Output Preview**:
   o Go to `Tools` > `Print Production` > `Output Preview`.
3. **Set the Correct Profile**:
   o In the Output Preview dialog box, set the `Simulation Profile` to match the embedded profile (e.g., Fogra 39, Fogra 51, GRACoL 2013).
   o This ensures that the colors are displayed as they will appear in the final printed output.

By following these steps, you ensure that your files adhere to industry-standard color profiles and that these profiles are preserved and embedded correctly in the PDF. This allows for accurate color representation across different viewing and printing platforms, maintaining the integrity of your designs. This process is crucial for professional print production, ensuring that the final output matches your design intentions accurately.

5.6 Calibrating Monitors and Printers

Calibration is a critical step in color management to ensure that the colors you see on your monitor match the colors printed on paper.

Picture 9. Monitor Calibration

- **Monitor Calibration**: Adjusting the monitor settings (brightness, contrast, color temperature) to match a known standard. This is typically done using a colorimeter or spectrophotometer. (Picture 9)
- **Printer Calibration**: Adjusting the printer settings to ensure the printed output matches the colors on the monitor. This involves using test prints and software to create an accurate color profile for the printer. (Picture 10)

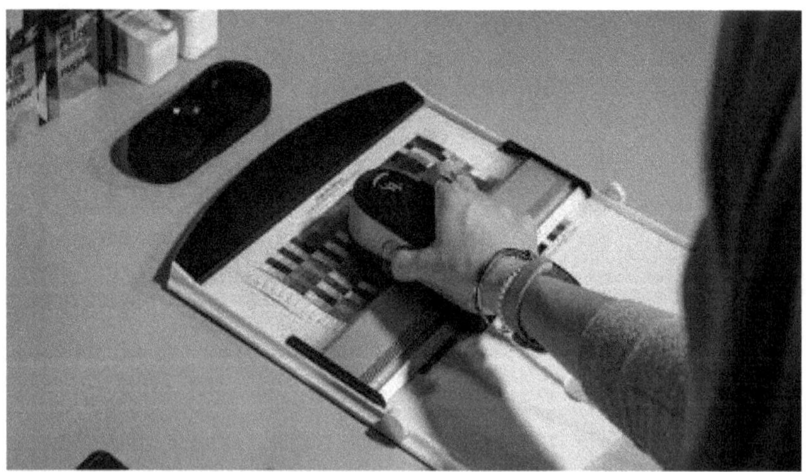

Picture 10. Printer Calibration using X-Rite i1Pro2

- **Calibration Tools**: Hardware devices and software applications used for calibration. Common tools include colorimeters, spectrophotometers, and calibration software like X-Rite i1Profiler or Datacolor Spyder.

Monitor Calibration Parameters as per Fogra

Fogra is a German-based research institute for media technologies, and its standards are widely respected in the printing and graphic arts industries. Key parameters according to Fogra standards include:

1. **Gamma**:
   o Typically set to a gamma of 2.2, which aligns with the natural response of the human eye to brightness.
2. **Color Rendering**:
   o Ensures accurate color reproduction by adhering to specific color spaces, such as sRGB or Adobe RGB.
3. **Illuminant**:
   o Use of standard illuminants like D50 for consistent color viewing conditions.
4. **White Point**:
   o Calibrated to match the standard D50 illuminant for consistency in white balance.

Calibration Process

1. **Measurement**:
   o The device (colorimeter or spectrophotometer) measures the monitor's current color output.
2. **Adjustment**:
   o The software adjusts the monitor's settings based on the measurements to match the desired standards (e.g., gamma, white point).
3. **Verification**:
   o Post-calibration, the device re-measures the output to ensure the adjustments were successful and meet the specified standards.

By adhering to these standards and using appropriate calibration devices, professionals can achieve accurate and consistent color reproduction across various platforms and media.

Ensuring Color Consistency

Maintaining color consistency is vital for professional-quality output, particularly in industries like photography, graphic design, and printing.

- **Soft Proofing**: A technique used to simulate how the final printed product will look on the screen. This helps in making necessary adjustments before printing.
- **Hard Proofing**: Creating a physical print proof to check the color accuracy and make any needed adjustments.
- **Consistent Lighting**: Using controlled lighting conditions while viewing and editing colors to ensure consistent perception of colors.
- **Color Spaces**: Understanding and working within the appropriate color space (e.g., sRGB, Adobe RGB, ProPhoto RGB) for your project to maintain color accuracy.
- **Regular Calibration**: Continuously calibrating your devices to account for any changes over time and maintain color accuracy.

In summary, mastering color management involves understanding color theory, using and creating accurate color profiles, regularly calibrating your devices, and employing techniques to ensure color consistency across different media.

5.7 Standard & Fixed Viewing Conditions

Achieving color consistency in printed images relies heavily on maintaining standard and fixed viewing conditions. Variations in ambient light can significantly alter the perceived color of a printed image, leading to discrepancies between the intended and observed colors.

Ambient light plays a crucial role in color perception. Changes in the light source, its intensity, or its color temperature can cause the same printed image to appear differently. For example, an image viewed under warm, yellowish indoor lighting will look different when viewed under cool, bluish daylight.

To mitigate the effects of changing ambient light, an in-house light booth is recommended (Picture 11). This controlled environment allows for consistent and standardized viewing conditions. A light booth simulates specific lighting conditions, ensuring that the colors seen are accurate and consistent, regardless of external lighting variations. Light booths in various sizes and models are available in the market. Now a day, all the production printers are providing the light booth along with the printer.

Picture 11. Light Booth

Recommended Light Sources for Color Consistency are mentioned below:

- **D50 (5000K) Daylight**: According to Fogra, an international research organization for media technologies, D50 lighting (5000 Kelvin) is the recommended standard for printing. This standard is part of ISO 3664, which specifies viewing conditions for the graphic technology and photography industries. D50 lighting closely replicates natural daylight at midday, providing a neutral and consistent light source for accurate color assessment.

- **D65 (6500K) Daylight**: While D50 is standard for the printing industry, D65 lighting (6500 Kelvin) is commonly used for industrial standards. D65 lighting simulates average daylight conditions, providing a slightly cooler light compared to D50. This is often used in industries where a broader range of lighting conditions is considered, such as in manufacturing and quality control.

Maintaining standard and fixed viewing conditions is essential for achieving color consistency in printed images. Using an in-house light booth with recommended lighting standards such as D50 for printing and D65 for industrial purposes ensures accurate and consistent color perception, minimizing the impact of ambient light variations.

6. IMPOSITION

6.1 The Basics of Imposition

Imposition is the process of arranging pages on a printer's sheet in a way that, after the sheet is folded, cut, and bound, the pages appear in the correct order. It is a critical step in the printing process that helps optimize paper usage, reduce waste, and improve print efficiency. (Picture 12), (Picture 13)

- **Purpose of Imposition**: Ensures that pages are in the correct order and orientation after printing, folding, and binding.
- **Imposition Layouts**: Different layouts are used depending on the type of binding and the size of the print run. Common layouts include 2-up, 4-up, 8-up, etc., which refer to the number of pages printed on a single sheet.

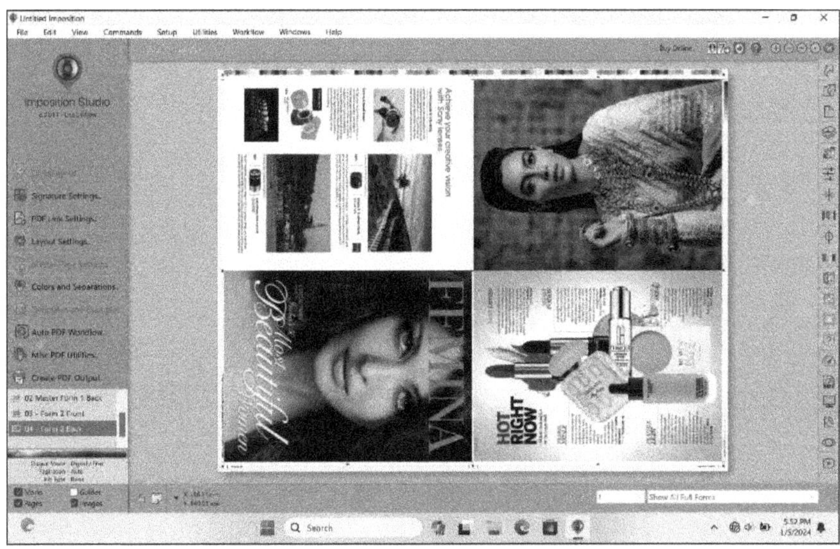

Picture 12. Imposition for Magazine/ Book Work

- **Folding Schemes**: The way a sheet is folded affects the imposition layout. Understanding different folding techniques is crucial for proper imposition.
- **Signature**: A group of pages that are printed on a single sheet of paper, which is then folded and cut to form a section of a book.

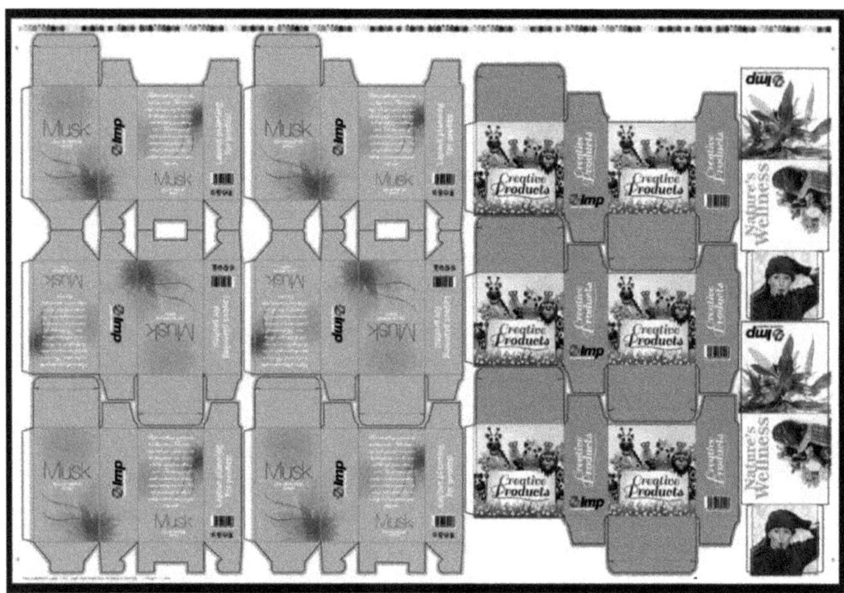

Picture 13. Imposition for packaging job – Folding Cartons

6.2 Types of Imposition: Saddle Stitch, Perfect Bound, etc.

Different binding methods require different imposition techniques. The choice of imposition type affects the overall design and layout of the printed material. (Picture 14)

- **Saddle Stitch**: Pages are folded and stapled along the spine. Imposition for saddle stitch requires pages to be arranged in a way that they nest within each other.

- **Perfect Bound**: Pages are stacked and glued along the spine. Imposition for perfect binding requires pages to be arranged sequentially since they are not nested.
- **Spiral Bound**: Pages are punched and bound using a spiral wire or plastic coil. Imposition is similar to perfect bound but may require adjustments for the binding margin.
- **Case Bound**: Similar to perfect bound but with a hardcover. Imposition needs to account for the additional spine and cover elements.
- **French Fold**: A sheet is printed on one side, folded twice to create four pages. Used for brochures and some special editions.

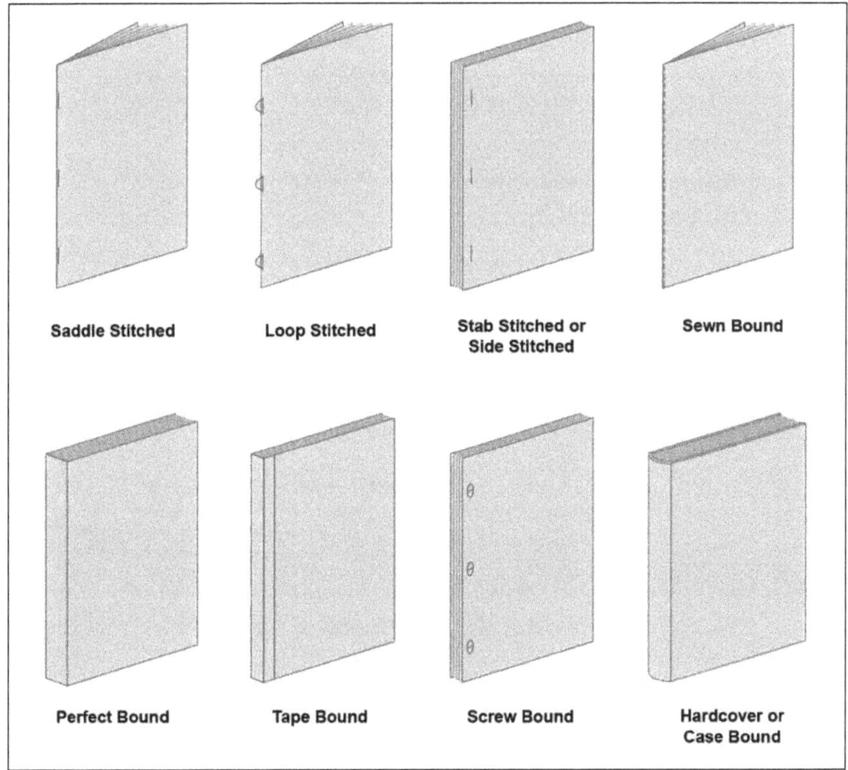

Picture 14. Different types of Bindings

6.3 Imposition Software and Tools

Imposition software automates the complex process of arranging pages for printing. These tools help designers and printers ensure accuracy and efficiency.

- **Adobe InDesign**: Offers built-in imposition tools and plugins for more advanced imposition tasks. Sometimes people are using Adobe Illustrator as well to do the imposition. These are mainly used in the digital on-demand printing industry.
- **QuarkXPress**: Another design software with imposition capabilities.
- **Preps (Kodak)**: A professional imposition software widely used in the printing industry. Preps comes with a wide range of features and solutions which can be customized very easily. This flexibility makes the software much useful and favorite to the finalizers and printing companies.
- **Impostrip (Ultimate TechnoGraphics)**: Known for its automation capabilities and flexibility in handling various imposition tasks.
- **Quite Imposing Plus**: A plugin for Adobe Acrobat that provides robust imposition features.

6.4 Best Practices for Imposition

Following best practices in imposition ensures high-quality printed materials and efficient production processes.

- **Plan Ahead**: Consider the final binding method and folding scheme during the design phase to avoid issues during imposition.
- **Use Templates**: Utilize imposition templates to streamline the process and maintain consistency across projects.
- **Check Bleeds and Margins**: Ensure that bleeds and margins are correctly set up to avoid issues with trimming and binding.

- **Proofing**: Always create and review proofs before the final print run to catch any errors in imposition.
- **Automation**: Use imposition software to automate repetitive tasks and reduce the risk of human error.
- **Collaboration**: Work closely with printers to understand their specific requirements and capabilities, ensuring that your imposition files meet their standards.
- **Quality Control**: Implement a thorough quality control process to check for issues like page order, orientation, and alignment.

In summary, imposition is a vital part of the printing process that requires careful planning and the right tools. Understanding the basics, choosing the appropriate type of imposition for the binding method, using specialized software, and following best practices will ensure that your printed materials are produced accurately and efficiently.

7. PREFLIGHTING

7.1 What is Preflighting?

Preflighting is the process of checking a digital document before it is sent to print or published. The goal is to ensure that the document is error-free and meets all necessary specifications for printing or digital distribution. Preflighting involves verifying various aspects such as fonts, colors, images, and layout to ensure that there are no issues that could affect the quality or accuracy of the final output.

7.2 Common Preflight Issues

1. **Missing Fonts**: When fonts used in the document are not embedded or included, it can lead to text appearing incorrectly.
2. **Low-Resolution Images**: Images that do not meet the required resolution can appear pixelated or blurry when printed. (Picture 15)
3. **Color Issues**: Incorrect color settings, such as using RGB instead of CMYK for print, can lead to color discrepancies.
4. **Bleed and Trim Errors**: Lack of proper bleed and trim settings can result in white borders or misaligned prints.
5. **Overprint Settings**: Incorrect overprint settings can cause certain elements to disappear or print incorrectly.
6. **Transparency Issues**: Problems with transparency can lead to unexpected results, such as missing or incorrectly rendered graphics.
7. **File Format Problems**: Using incorrect or incompatible file formats can prevent the document from being processed correctly by the printer.

Picture 15. Low resolution and High Resolution Images

7.3 Preflighting Software

Various software tools are available to assist with preflighting, each offering different features and capabilities:

1. **Adobe Acrobat Pro**: A widely used tool that provides comprehensive preflight checks and fixes for PDF documents. There are many standard preflight- profiles available in Adobe Acrobat Pro. Along with that we can create custom profiles to meet our quality standards and requirements.
2. **Enfocus PitStop Pro**: A powerful plugin for Adobe Acrobat that offers advanced preflight and editing capabilities. Enfocus Pitstop has its own standalone server & client software to automate the preflighting process. It helps the people and business owners to reduce the finalizing time and increase the efficiency of the existing system.

3. **FlightCheck by Markzware**: A standalone application that preflights a variety of file types, including PDFs, InDesign, and QuarkXPress files.
4. **Callas pdfToolbox**: A robust tool that offers automated preflighting and correction for PDF files.
5. **CorelDRAW**: Includes preflight tools specifically for checking documents created within the CorelDRAW environment.

7.4 Creating a Preflight Checklist

A preflight checklist ensures that all critical aspects of a document are reviewed and verified before final production. Here is an example checklist:

1. **Document Setup**:
   o Verify document size and orientation.
   o Check bleed and trim settings.
2. **Fonts and Text**:
   o Ensure all fonts are embedded or included.
   o Check for font substitutions or missing fonts.
   o Verify text alignment and spacing.
3. **Images and Graphics**:
   o Confirm image resolution meets requirements.
   o Check for missing or broken image links.
   o Verify correct color profiles (CMYK for print, RGB for digital).
4. **Colors and Inks**:
   o Ensure correct color settings (CMYK, spot colors).
   o Check for unnecessary spot colors.
   o Verify overprint settings.
5. **Layout and Design**:
   o Review layout for consistency and alignment.
   o Ensure all elements are within the safe area.
   o Check for unwanted elements or layers.

6. **File Format and Compatibility**:
    - o Save the document in the correct file format (PDF, EPS, etc.).
    - o Verify compatibility with the printer's requirements.
7. **Proofing**:
    - o Conduct a visual proof of the document.
    - o Print a test proof if possible.
    - o Review and approve the final document before sending it for production.

Creating a comprehensive preflight checklist helps to catch and correct potential issues early, saving time and resources while ensuring a high-quality final product.

8. TRAPPING

8.1 Understanding Trapping

Trapping is a prepress technique used to compensate for misregistration during the printing process. Misregistration occurs when different color plates or printing passes do not align perfectly, resulting in gaps or overlaps between colors. Trapping adjusts the boundaries of adjacent colors to create slight overlaps, ensuring that no white spaces (or unintended gaps) appear in the final printed piece. This technique is essential for maintaining the visual integrity and quality of printed materials, particularly in offset printing. (Picture 16)

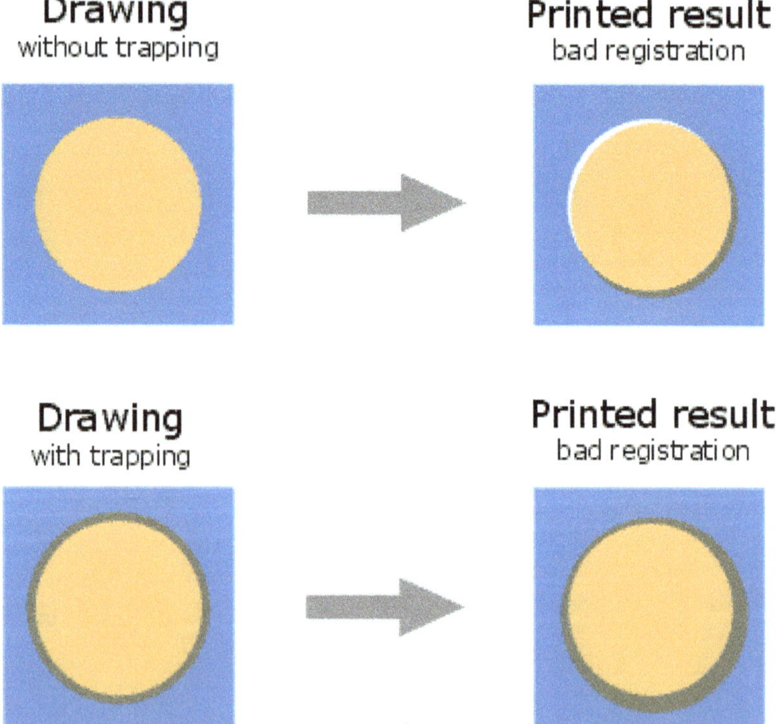

Picture 16. Artwork with trapping and without trapping

8.2 Types of Trapping: Spread, Choke, and Rich Black

1. **Spread**: Spread trapping involves slightly enlarging the lighter color to overlap into the adjacent darker color. This technique ensures that if there is any misregistration, the lighter color will spread into the darker color, preventing any gaps. (Picture 17)
2. **Choke**: Choke trapping is the opposite of spread trapping. It involves reducing the size of the darker color to allow the lighter color to overlap it slightly. This method is used when the lighter color needs to encroach upon the darker color to prevent gaps due to misregistration. (Picture 17)

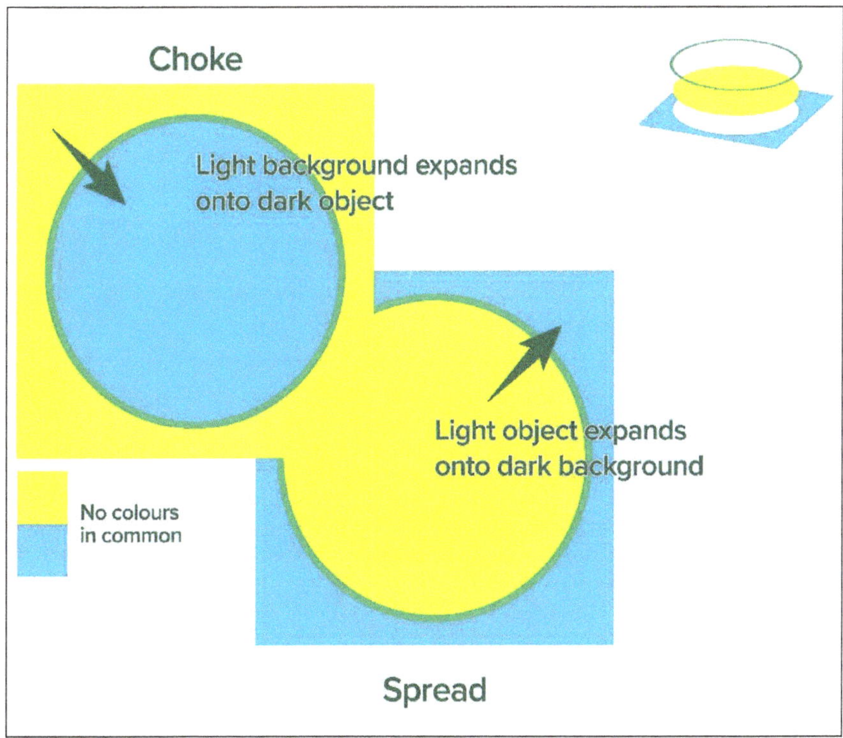

Picture 17. Types of Trapping - Choke & Spread

3. **Rich Black**: Rich black is a technique where black ink is overprinted with one or more colored inks (usually cyan, magenta, and yellow) to create a deep, intense black. This method ensures that the black areas appear solid and rich, and it also helps in preventing gaps between black and colored areas due to misregistration.

8.3 Automatic vs. Manual Trapping

1. **Automatic Trapping**: Modern prepress software often includes automatic trapping features. These tools analyze the document and apply the necessary trapping adjustments based on predefined settings and rules. Automatic trapping is efficient and can save significant time, especially for complex documents. However, it may not always produce the desired results for all types of artwork, particularly in cases with intricate designs or special printing requirements.
2. **Manual Trapping**: Manual trapping involves making trapping adjustments by hand, giving the designer or prepress technician complete control over the process. This method is often used for artwork with unique trapping needs or when the automatic trapping tools cannot achieve the required precision. While more time-consuming, manual trapping allows for customized solutions tailored to specific design and printing challenges.

8.4 Trapping Techniques and Tools

1. **Overprinting**: One of the simplest trapping techniques, overprinting involves printing one color directly over another. This technique is commonly used for trapping black text or elements over colored backgrounds, ensuring that any misregistration will not result in gaps.

2. **Knockout Trapping**: In knockout trapping, the underlying color is knocked out (removed) where the top color will be printed. Traps are then created around the edges of the knocked-out area to prevent gaps. This method is often used for more complex designs and when precise control over color overlaps is needed. (Picture 18)

Picture 18. Overprinting and Knockout

3. **Software Tools**:
   o **Adobe InDesign**: InDesign provides built-in trapping settings that allow users to apply automatic trapping to their documents. Users can also adjust trapping settings manually for more control.
   o **Adobe Illustrator**: Illustrator offers manual trapping options, enabling designers to adjust the overlap of colors directly within their artwork.
   o **Enfocus PitStop Pro**: A plugin for Adobe Acrobat, PitStop Pro includes advanced trapping tools that allow for both automatic and manual trapping adjustments.
   o **CorelDRAW**: CorelDRAW includes trapping tools that help users create and adjust traps for their vector artwork.
   o **Esko ArtPro+**: A prepress software specifically designed for packaging, ArtPro+ offers advanced trapping capabilities tailored for complex packaging designs.

4. **Proofing and Testing**: Before finalizing the trapping settings, it is essential to proof and test the document. Print test proofs to check for any misregistration issues and ensure that the traps are correctly applied. Adjust the trapping settings as needed based on the test results.

By understanding and effectively applying trapping techniques, designers and prepress technicians can ensure that their printed materials maintain high visual quality and consistency, even in the presence of minor misregistration during the printing process.

9. THE RIP PROCESS

9.1 What is a Raster Image Processor (RIP)?

A Raster Image Processor (RIP) is a specialized software or hardware that converts vector graphics, text, and images into raster (bitmap) images, which are then used by printers to produce the final printed output. The RIP process translates the digital file into a high-resolution grid of pixels or dots that the printer can interpret and print. This conversion is crucial for ensuring that the printed output matches the design's intended appearance, maintaining the quality and accuracy of the colors, images, and text. (Picture 19)

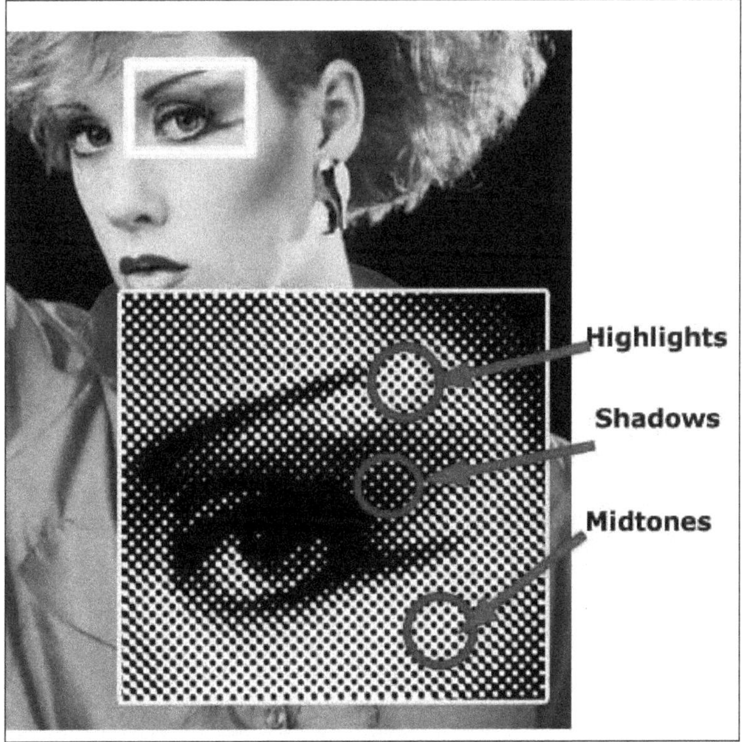

Picture 19. Image after Ripping - halftone

9.2 The RIP Workflow

The RIP workflow involves several steps to convert a digital document into a printable format:

1. **Input Processing**: The RIP software receives the digital file, typically in a format such as PDF, PostScript, or EPS. The file is analyzed to understand its components, including text, images, and vector graphics.
2. **Color Management**: The RIP processes the color information, ensuring that the colors in the digital file are accurately translated to the printer's color space. This step involves applying color profiles and performing color corrections to achieve the desired color output.
3. **Image Processing**: The RIP handles image scaling, resolution adjustments, and any necessary image enhancements or corrections. It ensures that all images are at the appropriate resolution for printing, typically 300 DPI or higher for high-quality output.
4. **Font Processing**: The RIP ensures that all fonts used in the document are available and properly rendered. It substitutes missing fonts with appropriate alternatives if necessary and embeds the fonts into the rasterized output.
5. **Rasterization**: The core function of the RIP is to convert vector graphics and text into raster images. This involves breaking down the digital file into a grid of pixels or dots that the printer can interpret and print.
6. **Output Generation**: The final rasterized image is prepared for printing. The RIP generates the necessary print files, often in formats such as TIFF, JPEG, or proprietary formats used by specific printers. These files are then sent to the printer for production.

9.3 Vector to Raster Conversion

Vector graphics are composed of paths defined by mathematical equations, making them resolution-independent and scalable without loss of quality. During the RIP process, these vectors are converted into raster images, which are resolution-dependent and consist of a grid of pixels. The conversion process involves:

1. **Antialiasing**: To smooth out the edges of vector shapes and text, the RIP applies antialiasing techniques. This reduces the jagged appearance of diagonal or curved lines by blending the edges with neighboring pixels.
2. **Resolution Adjustment**: The RIP determines the appropriate resolution for the raster image based on the printer's capabilities and the desired output quality. Higher resolutions result in more detailed and sharper images but also increase file size and processing time.
3. **Halftoning**: For printing processes that cannot reproduce continuous tones, such as offset printing, the RIP applies halftoning techniques. This involves creating a pattern of varying dot sizes and spacing to simulate different shades of color or grayscale. (Picture 19)

9.4 Handling Large Files and Complex Graphics

Managing large files and complex graphics during the RIP process requires careful consideration and optimization to ensure efficient processing and high-quality output:

1. **File Optimization**: Reduce the file size and complexity by optimizing images, flattening layers, and removing unnecessary elements. Use image compression techniques and ensure that all images are at the appropriate resolution for the intended print size.

2. **Memory Management**: The RIP software needs sufficient memory and processing power to handle large files and complex graphics. Ensure that the system running the RIP has adequate RAM and CPU resources to process the files efficiently.
3. **Incremental Processing**: Some RIP software can process large files in smaller segments or tiles. This approach reduces the memory load and allows for faster processing times, especially for large-format printing.
4. **Preflight Checks**: Perform preflight checks to identify and address potential issues before sending the file to the RIP. This includes verifying image resolutions, font embedding, color profiles, and overall file integrity.
5. **Parallel Processing**: Advanced RIP systems can utilize parallel processing techniques, distributing the workload across multiple processors or servers. This speeds up the RIP process and ensures timely production of large or complex print jobs.

By understanding the RIP process and effectively managing the conversion of vector graphics to raster images, designers and prepress technicians can ensure that their printed materials maintain high quality and accurately represent the intended design.

10. FINAL OUTPUT AND PRINTING

10.1 Preparing Files for Output

Preparing files for output involves several critical steps to ensure the document is ready for printing and meets the printer's specifications. Here's a detailed process:

1. **File Format**: Ensure the document is saved in the correct file format required by the printer. Common formats include PDF, EPS, TIFF, and JPEG. PDF is often preferred due to its ability to embed fonts and images. (Picture 20)
2. **Resolution**: Verify that all images and graphics are at the appropriate resolution, typically 300 DPI for high-quality print output. Lower resolutions can result in pixelated images.
3. **Color Mode**: Convert all colors to the appropriate color mode. For most print jobs, this is CMYK. Ensure any spot colors are correctly defined and named.
4. **Bleed and Trim**: Include bleed (typically 1/8 inch) around the document's edges to account for slight shifts during trimming. Ensure that important content is within the safe area, away from the trim line.
5. **Font Embedding**: Embed all fonts in the document to avoid font substitution issues. If embedding is not possible, outline the fonts.
6. **Image Links**: Check that all image links are updated and properly linked to the document. Missing or broken links can result in low-resolution prints. (Picture 20)
7. **Preflight Check**: Use preflight tools to verify the document for any potential issues, such as missing fonts, incorrect colors, or low-resolution images.

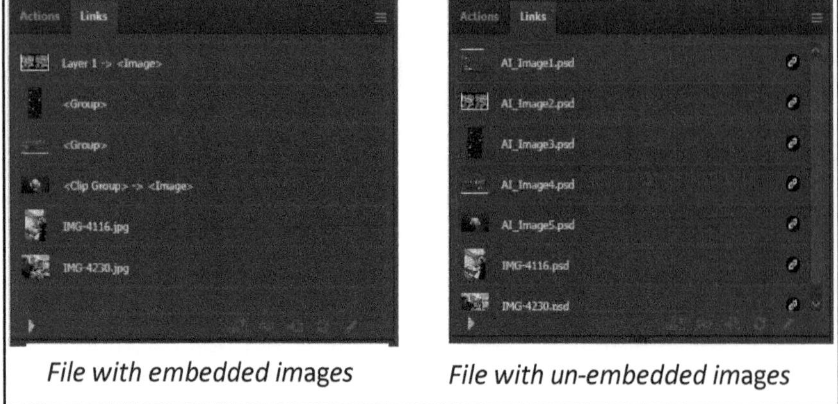

Picture 20. File with embedded and un-embedded images

10.2 Understanding Print Specifications

Understanding the print specifications is crucial for ensuring the final output meets the desired quality and standards. Key specifications include:

1. **Paper Type**: Specify the type of paper to be used, including weight, finish, and color. Options range from matte and glossy to coated and uncoated stocks.
2. **Printing Method**: Identify the printing method, such as offset, digital, screen, or flexographic printing. Each method has different requirements and capabilities.
3. **Color Specifications**: Define the color process, whether it's four-color process (CMYK), spot colors, or a combination. Provide Pantone or other color matching system references if necessary.
4. **Finishing**: Outline any finishing processes, such as binding, lamination, embossing, foil stamping, or die-cutting. These processes can affect file preparation.
5. **Quantity**: Specify the number of copies to be printed. This can impact cost and printing method selection.

6. **Size and Layout**: Confirm the document size and layout, including any special folds or configurations. Provide a mockup if needed.

10.3 Communicating with the Printer

Effective communication with the printer is essential for a successful print job. Key points of communication include:

1. **Detailed Job Specifications**: Provide a comprehensive job ticket with all the print specifications, including file format, color mode, paper type, and finishing requirements.
2. **Proof Approval**: Discuss proofing options, such as digital proofs or hardcopy proofs. Approve the proof to ensure the final output matches expectations.
3. **Timeline**: Establish a clear timeline for the project, including file submission, proofing, and final delivery dates. Ensure the printer can meet these deadlines.
4. **File Delivery**: Confirm the method for delivering files to the printer, whether via email, FTP, cloud storage, or physical media.
5. **Special Instructions**: Communicate any special instructions or considerations, such as handling sensitive materials or specific packaging requirements.
6. **Contact Information**: Provide contact details for both the client and the printer's point of contact to facilitate smooth communication and address any issues promptly.

10.4 Final Checks Before Printing

Before sending the final files to the printer, conduct thorough checks to ensure everything is in order:

1. **Content Review**: Double-check all text, images, and graphics for accuracy and completeness. Verify spelling, grammar, and alignment.
2. **Print Proof**: Review the print proof carefully. Check colors, resolution, and layout against the final design. Make any necessary adjustments based on the proof.
3. **Bleed and Margins**: Confirm that bleed and trim marks are correctly set up and that all important content is within the safe area.
4. **Color Consistency**: Ensure color consistency throughout the document. Use color profiles and proofing tools to match colors accurately.
5. **Page Order**: Verify the order of pages, especially for multi-page documents. Ensure any spreads or special layouts are correctly configured.
6. **File Integrity**: Check the final file for any corruption or errors. Ensure all fonts and images are embedded and linked correctly.
7. **Backup Files**: Create backups of the final files. This can save time and effort if any issues arise during the printing process.

By following these steps, you can ensure that your files are well-prepared for printing, meet all necessary specifications, and are communicated effectively to the printer. This process helps to achieve high-quality printed materials that match the intended design and requirements.

10.5. Different Printing Techniques

This chapter delves into various printing techniques foundational to the industry. Each method possesses unique characteristics, advantages, and preparation requirements. Understanding these techniques is vital for producing high-quality print outputs tailored to specific needs. Here, we provide a comprehensive overview of the following printing methods:

10.5.1. Offset Printing

Offset printing is a dominant method used for producing high-volume print runs with consistent quality. (Picture 21)

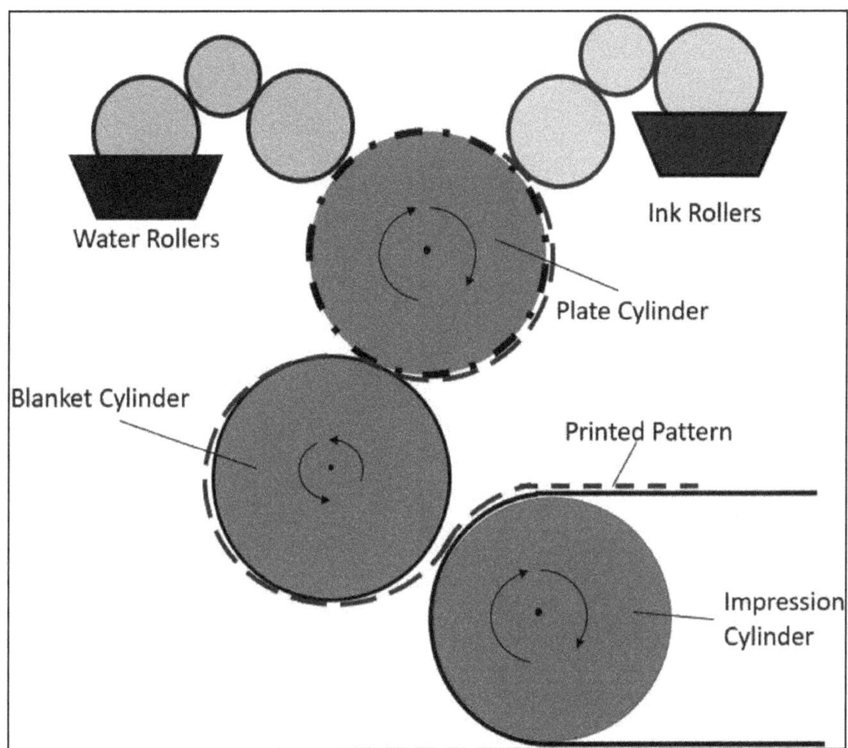

Picture 21. Offset Printing Process

- **Process Overview**: Offset printing involves transferring ink from a plate to a rubber blanket, then onto the printing surface. The process includes creating plates with the image to be printed, which are then mounted on a press.
- **File Preparation**:
    - **Resolution**: Ensure images are at least 300 DPI.
    - **Color Management**: Convert colors to CMYK and check color profiles.

- o **Bleed and Margins**: Include a 3mm bleed and maintain appropriate margins.
- **Advantages**: High image quality, cost-effective for large runs, and the ability to print on various paper types.
- **Applications**: Commonly used for books, magazines, newspapers, brochures, and stationery.

10.5.2. Flexography

Flexography is a versatile printing technique, especially popular for packaging. (Picture 22)

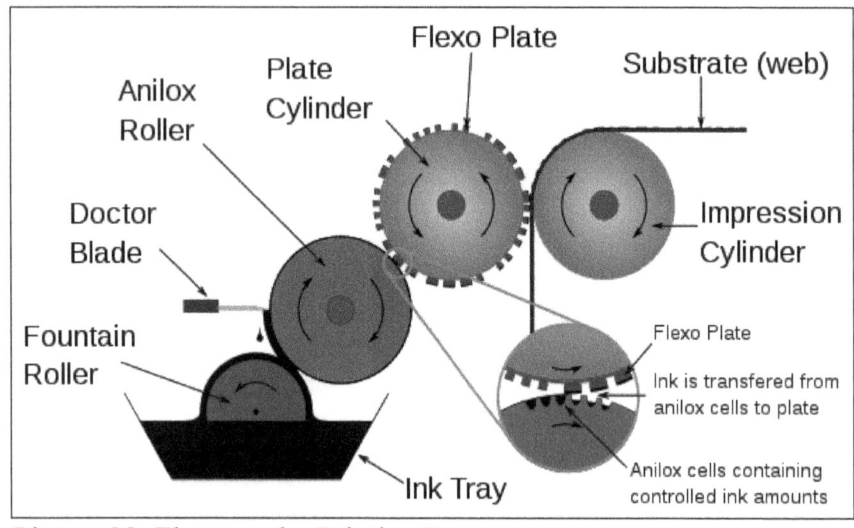

Picture 22. Flexography Printing Process

- **Process Overview**: Utilizes flexible relief plates and fast-drying inks. The ink is transferred from the plate directly to the substrate.
- **File Preparation**:
  - o **Resolution**: Maintain a resolution of 300 DPI or higher.

- o **Color Separations**: Properly separate colors and use trapping techniques to avoid misregistration.
  - o **Dot Gain Compensation**: Adjust for dot gain to ensure print accuracy.
- **Advantages**: Can print on a wide range of substrates, including plastics, foils, and paper. Ideal for continuous patterns.
- **Applications**: Used for food packaging, labels, corrugated containers, and wallpaper.

10.5.3. Gravure Printing

Gravure printing is known for producing high-quality images with fine detail. (Picture 23)

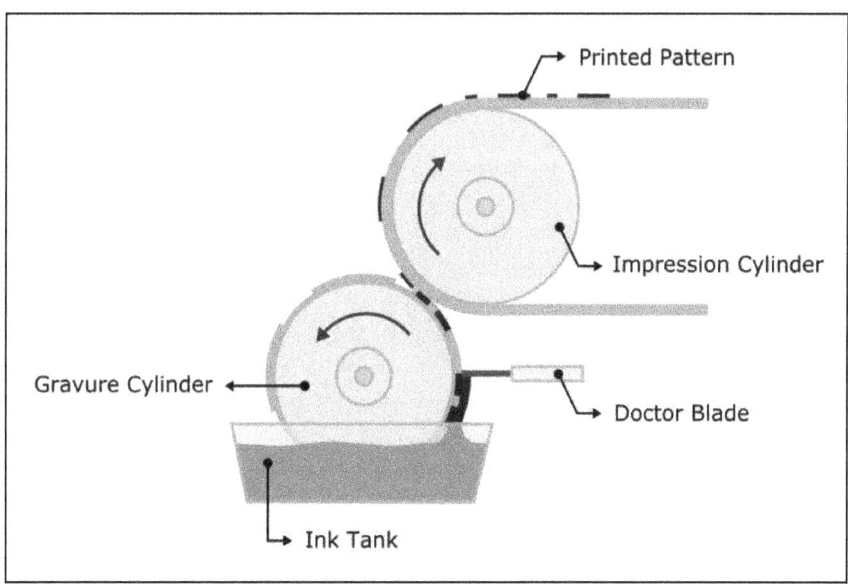

Picture 23. Gravure Printing Process

- **Process Overview**: Involves engraving the image onto a cylinder. The engraved areas are filled with ink, which is then transferred to the substrate.

- **File Preparation**:
  - **Resolution**: High-resolution images (at least 300 DPI) are essential.
  - **Continuous Tone Artwork**: Prepare files to handle smooth gradations.
  - **Color Management**: Ensure accurate color profiles and separations.
- **Advantages**: Excellent for long print runs and high-quality image reproduction.
- **Applications**: Magazines, catalogs, high-volume packaging, and specialty printing.

10.5.4. Digital Printing

Digital printing offers flexibility and is suitable for short runs and personalized prints.

- **Process Overview**: Uses digital files to print directly onto the substrate. Technologies include inkjet and laser printing.
- **File Preparation**:
  - **Resolution**: 300 DPI is recommended for clear prints.
  - **Color Profiles**: Use RGB or CMYK profiles depending on the printer specifications.
  - **File Formats**: Preferred formats include PDF, TIFF, and JPEG.
- **Advantages**: Quick setup, cost-effective for small quantities, allows for variable data printing.
- **Applications**: Personalized marketing materials, short-run books, posters, and direct mail.

10.5.5. Screen Printing

Screen printing is favored for printing on a variety of substrates, especially textiles. (Picture 24)

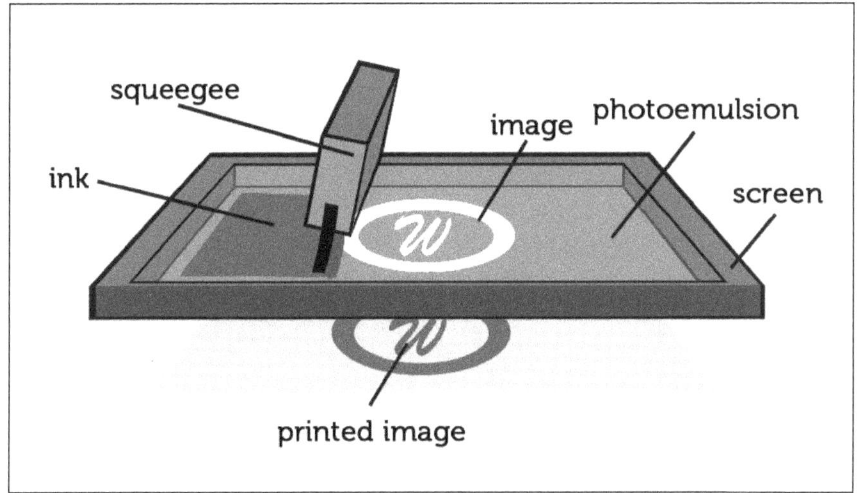

Picture 24. Screen Printing Process

- **Process Overview**: Involves creating a stencil (or screen) and using it to apply layers of ink onto the substrate.
- **File Preparation**:
    - **Vector Artwork**: Use vector files for crisp lines and shapes.
    - **Spot Colors**: Use spot colors to ensure color accuracy.
    - **Halftones**: Prepare halftones for images with gradients.
- **Advantages**: Versatile, can print on various materials, and suitable for large prints.
- **Applications**: T-shirts, posters, signs, and promotional items.

Preparing Files for Each Printing Method

Each printing technique has specific requirements for file preparation to ensure optimal results.

- **Resolution and Image Quality**: Recommendations for image resolutions to achieve sharp and clear prints.

- **Color Management**: Best practices for managing colors, including choosing the correct color spaces (CMYK or RGB), using spot colors, and ensuring consistent color profiles.
- **Bleed and Trim**: Instructions on setting up bleed areas and trim marks to ensure precise cutting and finishing of printed materials.
- **File Formats**: Preferred file formats (such as PDF, TIFF, EPS) and the necessary settings for each printing method to ensure compatibility and quality.

This knowledge is essential for selecting the most appropriate printing method for any project and managing the prepress process with confidence, ultimately leading to high-quality, professional print outputs.

11. CASE STUDIES AND REAL-WORLD APPLICATIONS

11.1 Case Study: Magazine Production

Background: A leading lifestyle magazine plans to release its quarterly issue, which includes high-quality images, detailed articles, and various advertisements.

Challenges:

- Ensuring high-quality print for images and text.
- Managing color consistency across different sections.
- Coordinating with multiple advertisers and contributors.
- Tight production deadlines.

Process:

1. **Content Collection**: Gather articles, images, and advertisements from contributors. Use a centralized platform for submission and feedback.
2. **Layout Design**: Use Adobe InDesign to create the magazine layout. Ensure consistent use of fonts, colors, and styles throughout the magazine.
3. **Preflighting**: Perform a thorough preflight check using Adobe Acrobat Pro to catch any issues such as missing fonts, low-resolution images, or incorrect color profiles.
4. **Proofing**: Produce digital proofs and a few hardcopy proofs to check the quality of images and text. Verify that all advertisements are correctly placed and rendered.
5. **RIP and Printing**: Convert the final layout to a high-resolution PDF and send it to the printer's RIP system. Ensure the printer's specifications are met, including CMYK color mode and appropriate resolution.

6. **Printing and Binding**: Print the magazine using offset printing. Apply binding techniques such as perfect binding or saddle stitching.

Outcome: The magazine was printed with vibrant colors, sharp images, and clear text. The tight coordination and rigorous proofing process ensured minimal errors, resulting in a high-quality publication that met the release deadline.

11.2 Case Study: Packaging Design

Background: A beverage company needs to redesign its packaging for a new product line, including labels, boxes, and promotional materials.

Challenges:

- Ensuring the design is eye-catching and aligns with brand identity.
- Managing color consistency across different packaging materials.
- Incorporating regulatory information and barcodes.
- Achieving high-quality print on various substrates.

Process:

1. **Design Concept**: Develop multiple design concepts using Adobe Illustrator. Incorporate brand colors, logos, and product information.
2. **Mockups and Prototypes**: Create digital mockups and physical prototypes to visualize the final packaging. Use 3D rendering software for realistic previews.
3. **Preflighting**: Use preflight tools to check for issues such as incorrect color profiles, missing fonts, and bleed settings. Ensure all elements meet regulatory requirements.

4. **Trapping and Color Management**: Apply trapping techniques to avoid misregistration issues. Use color management tools to ensure consistency across different materials and printing methods.
5. **RIP and Printing**: Prepare the final files and send them to the printer's RIP system. Print the labels, boxes, and promotional materials using a combination of offset and digital printing.
6. **Quality Control**: Conduct thorough quality checks on printed materials to ensure colors, text, and images are accurately reproduced. Verify that barcodes are scannable and regulatory information is clearly visible.

Outcome: The new packaging design was well-received, with vibrant colors and clear branding. The meticulous preflighting and trapping process ensured high-quality prints, while color management maintained consistency across different packaging materials.

11.3 Case Study: Large Format Printing

Background: An advertising agency needs to produce a series of large-format banners and posters for a national marketing campaign.

Challenges:

- Ensuring high resolution and image quality at large sizes.
- Managing color accuracy and consistency.
- Handling large file sizes and complex graphics.
- Meeting tight production deadlines.

Process:

1. **Design and Layout**: Create designs using Adobe Photoshop and Illustrator. Ensure all images and graphics are high resolution and suitable for large-scale printing.
2. **Preflighting**: Use preflight tools to check for potential issues such as low-resolution images, incorrect color profiles, and bleed settings. Ensure all files are optimized for large-format printing.
3. **File Management**: Manage large file sizes by using efficient file formats (e.g., TIFF) and compressing images without losing quality. Use a powerful computer system with adequate RAM and processing power.
4. **RIP and Printing**: Prepare the files for the RIP system, ensuring high resolution and correct color profiles. Print the banners and posters using large-format printers, such as inkjet or solvent printers.
5. **Quality Control**: Conduct detailed inspections of the printed banners and posters to ensure image clarity, color accuracy, and overall quality. Make adjustments if necessary and reprint any flawed pieces.

Outcome: The large-format banners and posters were produced with exceptional quality, featuring sharp images and vibrant colors. The campaign materials effectively captured attention and conveyed the desired message, contributing to the campaign's success.

11.4 Lessons Learned and Best Practices

1. Rigorous Preflighting: Always perform thorough preflight checks to catch issues early and avoid costly reprints. Use professional preflighting tools and involve multiple team members for review.

2. Effective Communication: Maintain clear and consistent communication with printers, contributors, and clients. Provide detailed job specifications and promptly address any questions or concerns.

3. Color Management: Use color management tools and techniques to ensure color consistency across different materials and printing methods. Regularly calibrate monitors and proofing devices.

4. File Optimization: Optimize files for their intended use, managing resolution, file size, and format. Ensure that all images, fonts, and links are correctly embedded and updated.

5. Proofing and Testing: Always review proofs carefully, both digital and hardcopy, to ensure the final output matches the intended design. Conduct test prints when working with new materials or printing methods.

6. Backup and Redundancy: Keep multiple backups of final files and project assets. This ensures that work is not lost and can be quickly recovered in case of technical issues.

7. Continuous Learning: Stay updated with the latest industry trends, tools, and technologies. Regularly attend workshops, webinars, and training sessions to enhance skills and knowledge.

By following these lessons learned and best practices, designers and prepress technicians can improve their processes, achieve higher quality outputs, and effectively manage complex print projects.

12. FUTURE TRENDS IN PREPRESS

12.1 Automation and AI in Prepress

Automation: Automation is increasingly streamlining prepress workflows, reducing manual intervention, and improving efficiency. Key areas include:

- **Preflighting and Correction**: Automated preflight tools can quickly identify and fix common issues like missing fonts, low-resolution images, and incorrect color profiles. These tools can save significant time and reduce human error.
- **Job Setup and Imposition**: Automated systems can handle tasks like job setup, imposition (arranging pages for printing), and applying necessary trapping. This ensures consistent quality and faster turnaround times.
- **Variable Data Printing (VDP)**: Automation enables efficient handling of VDP, where each printed piece can be customized with unique text, images, or graphics without manual setup for each variation.

Artificial Intelligence (AI): AI is transforming prepress by offering advanced capabilities:

- **Image Recognition and Enhancement**: AI-powered tools can analyze images, identify issues, and automatically enhance them for better print quality. This includes tasks like noise reduction, sharpening, and color correction.
- **Predictive Maintenance**: AI can predict when printing equipment might fail or need maintenance, reducing downtime and improving productivity.
- **Smart Proofing**: AI can simulate how different substrates and printing conditions will affect the final output, allowing for more accurate proofing and adjustments.

12.2 Advances in Proofing Technologies

Digital Proofing: Digital proofing technologies continue to evolve, offering more accurate and efficient ways to preview and adjust designs before printing:

- **Soft Proofing**: High-quality monitors and color calibration tools allow for precise soft proofing, where designers can view accurate representations of the final print on screen. This reduces the need for physical proofs and speeds up the approval process.
- **Remote Proofing**: Advances in internet speeds and cloud-based tools enable remote proofing, allowing stakeholders to review and approve proofs from anywhere. This is particularly useful for global teams and clients.

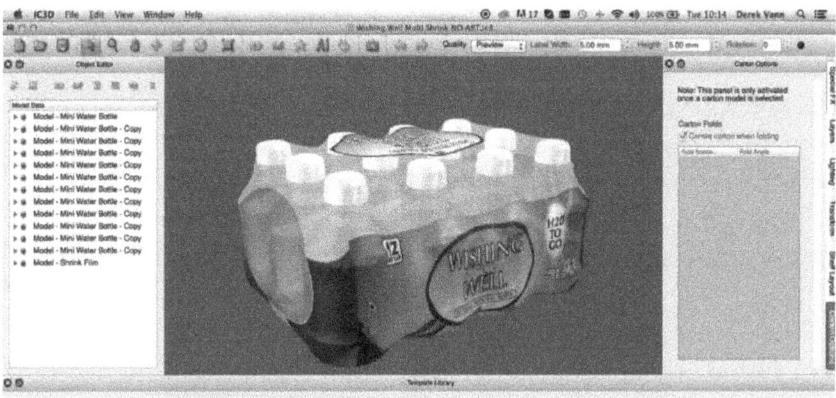

Picture 25. 3D Digital Mockup made using ic3D software

- **3D Proofing**: For packaging and other three-dimensional projects, 3D proofing tools provide realistic visualizations of how the final product will look. This includes folding, die-cuts, and other structural elements. (Picture 25)

Color Proofing: Color proofing technologies are improving, ensuring that the colors seen in proofs match the final printed output more accurately:

- **Spectrophotometers**: These devices measure color accurately and are used in conjunction with proofing systems to ensure color fidelity.
- **Advanced Color Management Systems**: These systems integrate with proofing tools to manage color profiles and simulate different printing conditions, ensuring consistent color reproduction across various media and devices.

12.3 The Role of Cloud Computing in Prepress

Collaboration and File Sharing: Cloud computing facilitates seamless collaboration and file sharing among teams, clients, and printers:

- **Real-Time Collaboration**: Cloud-based tools allow multiple users to work on the same document simultaneously, making it easier to coordinate changes and updates in real-time.
- **Version Control**: Cloud platforms provide version control, ensuring that all stakeholders are working on the latest version of a document. This reduces errors and miscommunication.

Scalability and Accessibility: Cloud computing offers scalability and accessibility benefits for prepress operations:

- **Scalable Resources**: Cloud services can scale resources up or down based on project needs, offering flexibility and cost savings.
- **Remote Access**: Teams can access prepress tools and files from any location with internet connectivity, enabling remote work and reducing the need for physical infrastructure.

Data Security and Backup: Cloud providers offer robust security and backup solutions:

- **Data Security**: Advanced encryption and security protocols protect sensitive files and information from unauthorized access.
- **Automatic Backup**: Cloud services automatically back up data, reducing the risk of data loss due to hardware failures or other issues.

12.4 Sustainable Practices in Prepress and Printing

Eco-Friendly Materials: The industry is shifting towards more sustainable materials:

- **Recycled Paper and Inks**: Using recycled paper and eco-friendly inks reduces the environmental impact of printing. Soy-based and vegetable-based inks are popular alternatives to traditional petroleum-based inks.
- **Biodegradable Substrates**: For packaging and other printed materials, biodegradable substrates offer an environmentally friendly option that reduces waste.

Energy-Efficient Technologies: Advances in printing technology are focusing on energy efficiency:

- **Digital Printing**: Digital printing technologies often use less energy and produce less waste compared to traditional offset printing, making them a more sustainable choice for short runs and on-demand printing.
- **Energy-Efficient Equipment**: Newer printing presses and prepress equipment are designed to be more energy-efficient, reducing the overall carbon footprint of the printing process.

Waste Reduction: Implementing practices to reduce waste is becoming a priority:

- **Optimized Imposition**: Using software to optimize imposition reduces paper waste by maximizing the use of available space on each sheet.
- **Recycling Programs**: Establishing comprehensive recycling programs for paper, ink cartridges, and other materials helps reduce waste and promote sustainability.

Sustainable Workflows: Developing sustainable workflows involves integrating eco-friendly practices at every stage:

- **Green Certifications**: Seeking certifications like FSC (Forest Stewardship Council) or SFI (Sustainable Forestry Initiative) ensures that materials come from responsibly managed forests.
- **Lean Manufacturing**: Implementing lean manufacturing principles helps minimize waste, improve efficiency, and reduce the environmental impact of printing processes.

By embracing these future trends, the prepress and printing industry can enhance efficiency, improve quality, and promote sustainability, ultimately leading to better outcomes for both businesses and the environment.

GLOSSARY: DEFINITIONS OF COMMON PREPRESS TERMS

- **Bleed**: An extra margin around the edges of a document to ensure that no unprinted edges occur in the final trimmed document.
- **Choke**: A trapping technique where the lighter background color is reduced to let the darker foreground color spread into it.
- **CMYK**: Cyan, Magenta, Yellow, and Key (Black) - the color model used in color printing.
- **Color Profile**: A set of data that characterizes a color input or output device, or a color space, according to standards by the International Color Consortium (ICC).
- **DPI**: Dots Per Inch - a measure of spatial printing or video dot density.
- **Font Embedding**: Including font files within a document to ensure consistent text appearance across different systems.
- **Imposition**: The arrangement of pages on a printer's sheet to ensure that they are in the correct order after folding and binding.
- **Knockout**: A method in printing where the bottom color is not printed under the top color to prevent mixing.
- **Overprinting**: Printing one color over another to prevent gaps and ensure colors blend correctly.
- **Preflight**: The process of checking a digital document for errors before printing.
- **Raster Image Processor (RIP)**: A component used in a printing system to produce a raster image also known as a bitmap.
- **Resolution**: The amount of detail an image holds, measured in DPI for print.
- **RGB**: Red, Green, Blue - the color model used for digital screens.

- **Spread**: A trapping technique where the lighter color spreads into the darker color to avoid gaps.
- **Vector Graphics**: Graphics based on mathematical equations that allow for infinite scalability without loss of quality.

APPENDICES

Appendix A: Prepress Software and Tools

1. **Adobe Creative Suite**
   - **Adobe InDesign**: Professional layout and page design software for print and digital media.
   - **Adobe Illustrator**: Vector graphics editor and design program.
   - **Adobe Photoshop**: Image editing and photo retouching software.
   - **Adobe Acrobat Pro**: PDF creation, editing, and preflighting tool.
2. **QuarkXPress**: A desktop publishing software for creating and editing complex page layouts.
3. **CorelDRAW**: A vector graphics editor used for design and layout tasks.
4. **Enfocus PitStop Pro**: A PDF preflight, editing, and correction tool.
5. **Esko ArtPro+**: A PDF editor specifically designed for packaging prepress.
6. **Kodak Prinergy**: Workflow management software for prepress processes.
7. **Agfa Apogee**: A prepress workflow automation software suite.
8. **EFI Fiery**: A digital front-end system for high-performance digital printing.

Appendix B: Useful Resources and Further Reading

1. **Books**:
   - "Real World Print Production with Adobe Creative Suite Applications" by Claudia McCue.
   - "The Non-Designer's Design Book" by Robin Williams.

- o "Adobe InDesign CC Classroom in a Book" by Kelly Kordes Anton and Tina DeJarld.
2. **Websites**:
   - o <u>PrintWiki</u>: The Free Encyclopedia of Print.
   - o <u>WhatTheyThink</u>: Industry news and analysis.
   - o <u>CreativePro</u>: Resources for creative professionals.
3. **Organizations**:
   - o **Printing Industries of America**: Offers resources and advocacy for the printing industry.
   - o **The International Color Consortium (ICC)**: Develops and promotes the use of open, vendor-neutral, cross-platform color management systems.

Appendix C: Sample Preflight Checklist

1. **Document Setup**:
   - ☐ Correct page size and orientation.
   - ☐ Bleed and trim marks included.
   - ☐ Safe area margins checked.
2. **Images**:
   - ☐ All images at 300 DPI or higher.
   - ☐ CMYK color mode.
   - ☐ Linked images updated and embedded.
3. **Fonts**:
   - ☐ All fonts embedded or outlined.
   - ☐ Font sizes and styles consistent.
4. **Colors**:
   - ☐ Colors converted to CMYK.
   - ☐ Spot colors properly defined and named.
5. **Text**:
   - ☐ Spelling and grammar checked.

☐ Text properly aligned and formatted.

6. **Graphics**:

    ☐ Vector graphics checked for resolution.

    ☐ Trapping settings applied where necessary.

7. **Proofing**:

    ☐ Digital proofs reviewed.

    ☐ Hardcopy proofs checked for color accuracy.

8. **File Integrity**:

    ☐ Final file saved in correct format (e.g., PDF).

    ☐ Preflight check performed using preflight software.

    ☐ Backup of final files created.

By utilizing these tools, resources, and checklists, prepress professionals can ensure that their print projects are executed smoothly and to the highest quality standards.